A 21st Century Road Trip:

One Traveler's Thoughts on People, Places, Corvettes, & the Open American Road
John Mulhern III

Copyright © 2006 by John Mulhern III.
All rights reserved.
This book may not be reproduced, in whole or in part, including illustrations, in any form (beyond that copying permitted by Sections 107 and 108 of U.S. Copyright Law and except by reviewers for the public press), without written permission from the author.

Designed by John Mulhern III
Set in Adobe Garamond Pro and Adobe Myriad Pro type by John Mulhern III.

To my wonderful wife Ivelis, without whom even consideration of this trip or this book would have been impossible.

Table of Contents

Author's Note	vii

Introduction & Prelude   ix
    "No, What Do You Want?" • I Married The Right Woman • Option R8C •
    Our Little Red Corvette • *Grace* • 'Corvette Heaven' • Test Runs
    [Sidebars: The Corvette Generations, What Did It Come With?,
    Planning & Deciding On The Route]

1 Leg One: Bryn Mawr, PA to Chicago, IL   1
    Heading Out • *Grace* Sees Snow • Advantages Of A Big City
    [Sidebars: Gilding The Lily?, Where To Stay?]

2 Leg Two, Part I: Chicago, IL to Tucumcari, NM on Route 66   7
    Picking Up Route 66 • Millenium Yellow Makes An Appearance •
    Journey To The Top • A Short Excursion In Kansas •
    A Whale, An Ark, & A Round Barn • More Treasures Along The Route •
    The Cadillac Ranch • 'Tucumcari Tonite'
    [Sidebar: Packing & Laundry]

3 Leg Two, Part II: Tucumcari, NM to Santa Monica, CA on Route 66   21
    Sante Fe: The City Different • Ivelis Gets Her Boots • The Geronimo Legend •
    "¡Pricessa De Puerto Rico Levantaste Y Bailé!" •
    Top Down In The Petrified Forest • Green Dinosaurs In Holbrook •
    Celebrating Our Wedding Anniversary In Kingman, AZ •
    Breakfast At Mr. D'z • Negotiating The Twisties, Then & Now •
    Old Route 66 In California
    [Sidebars: Getting Out & About, What's Different About A Convertible]

4 Leg Three: Santa Monica, CA to Seattle, WA on the Pacific Coast Highway   35
    Meeting Up With Andy & Tamiza • Automotive Eye Candy •
    Catching Up With Kevin • Joining An Impromptu Caravan •
    Bread, Rum, & Coke • Where I Found *Lauren*
    [Sidebars: The Corvette Sub-Cultures, My Other Corvette, The Electronics]

5 Leg Four, Part I: Seattle, WA to Des Moines, IA   47
    Heading Back East • *Grace* Sees Snow … Again •
    Restoring *Grace* To Respectability • Magnificent Mount Rushmore •
    Wall Drug, Wall Drug, Wall Drug • Dining At Rosie's • Renaissance Romance
    [Sidebars: Eating Our Way Across The USA, The Beauty Of America,
    Hotels With A History]

6 Leg Four, Part II: Des Moines, IA to Bryn Mawr, PA   55
    Last Leg • Impressive Indianapolis • Familiar Territory • Home Sweet Home
    [Sidebar: Preparing For Road Emergencies]

Table of Contents

Appendix One: Lists   **61**
    Best Of The Trip • Memorable Moments •
    Post Script: What's Happened Since The Trip • Music To Drive By •
    What Was On Our iPod

Appendix Two: Annotated Bibliography   **67**

Appendix Three: Photograph & Graphic Credits   **69**

Author's Note

I wrote this book because I wanted to tell the story of our trip in April 2005, both because I thought that other people would find it interesting and amusing and because I didn't want to let time fade away any of the details of the trip.

I wanted this book to work both for Corvette people and for people who know nothing or next to nothing about Corvettes. So, there are explanations of some Corvette things that many Corvette people may find more than a bit basic and that some non-Corvette people may find far too extensive. I hope the reader will forgive this inability to leave an explanation out.

Acknowledgments & Thanks

First, thanks to my wife Ivelis, for her assistance, support, understanding, and most of all, her love.

Thanks to Celeste Stewart, who made lengthy and long-suffering attempts at editing this much-revised manuscript. Any slip-ups that missed her eagle eye are mine alone.

Thanks to Erin Flannery for fact checking help.

Thanks to Richard Banker, Dwayne Fenton, Lynda Simonetti, Etienne Vanaret, and Matthew Wallop for assistance in securing photographs.

Thanks to the folks on Corvette Forum and on FerrariChat for information, fact checking, and (patient) assistance.

Introduction & Prelude

"No, What Do You Want?"

Planning for this trip began shortly after our first Route 66 trip in April 2000 (our fifth wedding anniversary). We had performed that trip in our 1999 Chrysler 300M (our daily driver and our only car at the time). It had been a blast, but we had learned so much about Route 66 during that trip that we wanted to travel the same route again.

April 2000: Ivelis in our 1999 Chrysler 300M in the Petrified Forest National Park, AZ

Getting a *Corvette* for this trip, however, can be attributed to our financial advisor, Jim Izzo. We were having our annual review meeting with him and he asked me "What do you want?"—a somewhat open-ended question. I gave him work-related answers such as growing my business, continuing to expand my client base, and identifying profitable specialties. Jim said, "No, what do *you* want?" It got me thinking … within a couple of weeks I had decided that I wanted a Corvette, but I did not instantly decide on which one. At first I thought that we might get a late 1980s or early 1990s Corvette convertible, at that time one generation old.

I Married The Right Woman

In August 2000, I purchased *All Corvettes Are Red*, a book by James Shefter—ACAR, as it is known to Corvette folks. This book is the story of the C5, the fifth-generation Corvette. While there is some disagreement among Corvette fans about some of Shefter's specifics, there is total agreement about how amazing the basic story is. *All Corvettes Are Red* convinced me that I wanted a C5, and I think Ivelis was willing to be convinced, too.

The Corvette Generations

The various Corvette generations are often designated by C1 through C6, though this is a relatively recent practice—generations were previously identified differently by the Corvette cognicenti. The generations are generally agreed to be:

C1 (1953-1962)—the first Corvettes, often called 'solid-axles' because they're the only Corvettes without an independent rear suspension. These Corvettes changed vastly between 1953 and 1962, gaining much-needed V8s in 1955, and both fuel injection and 4-speed manual transmissions in 1957

C2 (1963-1967)—a complete redesign, the Sting Rays, also called 'mid-years', these were the first Corvettes with independent rear suspension, rotating headlights, and (in 1965) four wheel disk brakes. In 2004, Automobile magazine called the 1967 Sting Ray the "coolest car in history"

C3 (1968-1982)—often called 'sharks', these were initially derided as merely a styling change but ended up much loved, getting the Corvette through the tenuous and low-performance mid-1970s and modernization in the late 1970s and early 1980s

C4 (1984-1996)—a long overdue complete redesign from the 'sharks', these were arguably the first modern Corvettes, being the first Corvettes to have anti-lock brakes, 6-speed manual transmissions, traction control, and air bags

C5 (1997-2004)—another complete redesign, designed from the ground up for exotic car performance in an easy-to-maintain package

C6 (2005-?)—the latest Corvettes and the fastest stock versions ever, not quite a complete redesign like the C4 or C5, but full of useful enhancements and refinements

Introduction & Prelude

The immensely motivating 'refrigerator' shot from the 2001 Corvette brochure

Shortly after reading *All Corvettes Are Red*, I downloaded the 2001 Corvette brochure in Acrobat/PDF format from the Chevrolet web site. One of the double page 'beauty shots' in the brochure is a drawing of a red Corvette convertible in front of some large industrial fans. I printed this picture out for Ivelis on our Epson inkjet photo printer. She put it up on the refrigerator in our kitchen, where it stayed as a constant motivational reminder.

In early 2002, Ivelis told me that we could purchase a Corvette. I looked at her more than a bit incredulously—"Do you know how much a new Corvette costs?", I said. "Yes." she said, as if this was a completely irrelevant and somewhat silly question. Things like this serve to remind me that I married the right woman.

For most major purchases in our marriage, Ivelis chooses the basic specifications and I work on the details. In the case of the Corvette it was no different. Ivelis told me the Corvette had to meet these specifications:

- be some shade of red
- be a convertible
- have an automatic transmission

We have since taken a lot of ribbing about the automatic transmission, but as Ivelis says, she kills clutches (both of us have looked with some considerable lust at the paddle shifting six-speed automatic newly available on the 2006 C6 Corvettes).

As I started to look around, the idea that we were actually going to get a Corvette became more real and I started to become a lot more specific about what I wanted vis-a-vis Ivelis' specifications.

Option R8C

In April 2002, Chevrolet announced the 50th Anniversary Edition convertibles and coupes. These cars, with their special paint, badging, and 'trick' magnetic ride, had instantaneous appeal to us. I know myself and I knew that I would always want to have the latest and greatest—the 50th Anniversary Edition would always be special, so I would (hopefully) be able to restrain myself at least a little bit from moving on to the next Corvette generation as soon as it became available.

The astonishing thing about this whole process is that we never took a test drive of *any* C5 Corvette before purchasing our particular model. For various reasons, we had confidence that the Corvette was going to be a great car. Luckily, that confidence was well rewarded—our Corvette has exceeded all of our (very high) expectations.

We purchased our Corvette over the Internet, buying from Maxie Price Chevrolet in Augusta, Georgia, one of the largest Corvette dealers in the nation. After flying down from Philadelphia, PA to Nashville, TN (the closest large airport), we rented a car and drove up to Bowling Green, KY.

We took what is called museum delivery (option R8C) at the National Corvette Museum (which is cleverly and conveniently located across the street from the Corvette plant) on April 25th, 2003.

For any Corvette person, museum delivery is an incredible experience. First, the new owner gets an individualized tour of the Corvette plant —spectacular and interesting in its own right. Then there's a backstage tour of the museum which finishes at your new Corvette, which is parked on the museum floor. The actual car delivery process happens right then and there—the guide demonstrates all the features and capabilities of your new Corvette as museum visitors walk by and stare!

After the delivery process was complete, we had our picture taken with the Corvette Chief Engineer, Dave Hill and asked him to sign the car—it's fairly common to ask the Chief Engineer involved in designing your version of the Corvette to sign some part of it (he signed the underside of the hood with metallic markers he carries for that purpose).

What Did It Come With?

By 2003, Chevrolet had made a lot of equipment that had been optional or unavailable when the C5 was introduced in 1997 standard. Any Corvette convertible in 2003 came with a 350 horsepower engine, active handling, four-wheel anti-lock disc brakes, a fully independent suspension, speed sensitive power steering, and traction control. Inside, there was a multitude of comfort and convenience items: dual-zone air conditioning and heating (fairly decadant in a two seater), cruise control, power door locks, power windows, tilt steering wheel, remote keyless entry, and six-way power seats for both driver and passenger (the most comfortable seats that I have ever been in—inside or outside of a car).

In order to move several steps beyond what came standard on every 2003 Corvette convertible, Chevrolet made sure that the 50th Anniversary Editions only came loaded. So, when we checked off the Anniversary Edition box, we also got the F55 magnetic ride (an amazing compromise between ride and handling with two available settings), heads-up display (speed, tachometer, and other information is projected on the windshield), power telescoping steering column, a comprehensive memory package (it remembers settings for the outside mirrors, air conditioning/heater/defogger, stereo, driver seat, and telescoping steering column), and twilight sentinel (the headlights come on automatically when it gets dark).

We carefully configured our 50th Anniversary Edition convertible (we soon learned that Corvette shorthand for one like ours is 'AE 'vert'), though there weren't many options left to choose. We checked off the aforementioned automatic transmission, museum delivery, the in-dash cassette player with 12-CD changer in the trunk, and the body side moldings.

Introduction & Prelude

April 2003: picking up the Corvette at the Corvette Museum in Bowling Green, KY— that's Dave Hill, Corvette Chief Engineer, on the left & two fairly dazed folks on the right

Our Little Red Corvette

More than a little dazed from the whole delivery experience, we drove off into the sunset, with the top down and Prince's *Little Red Corvette* playing on the stereo—I had burned a set of music CDs specifically for the occasion and *Little Red Corvette* was the first song on the first CD, built (you guessed it!) to Ivelis' basic specification.

Planning & Deciding On The Route

When we started to plan our route, we had several constraints. First, we had to complete the entire trip within a set amount of time—we couldn't reasonably set aside an entire month for this vacation. Second, we had locational requirements; there were places we wanted to visit again (Chicago, the Oklahoma Route 66 Museum, Santa Fe, etc.) and places that we wanted to visit as a couple for the first time (the Pro Football Hall of Fame, San Francisco, Seattle, Mount Rushmore, etc.). Finally, there were also friends we wanted to see in California (Andy Bogus in the Los Angeles area and Kevin O'Connor in the San Luis Obispo area).

With all this in mind, I started to lay out a route about a year before our trip began. This route changed in detail and timing many times, but the basics stayed the same: a quick run out to Chicago, the entire length of Route 66, significant portions of the Pacific Coast Highway, and then back on the interstates from the northwest to the northeast with an all-important stop in South Dakota to see 'the presidents'.

As we drove toward our stop for the night in Louisville, KY that evening, it began to get markedly more chilly. We pulled over by the side of the road to put the top up and resumed our trip. About five minutes later, we drove into an absolutely torrential rainstorm. At that point I thought "Oh no ... what if it leaks?" (many older Corvette convertibles are known for their leaks). But our beautiful new convertible stayed warm and dry and got us safely to the lovely old Camberly Brown Hotel in Louisville that night. We drove home over the next two days, staying at the Omni William Penn Hotel in Pittsburgh, PA (another neat old hotel) the following night and making a stop at Frank Lloyd Wright's Fallingwater house in Bear Run, PA before heading home.

Grace

We named our new Corvette *Grace* (it's a bit of an Ivelis and John foible, but I'll admit that we name all our cars). Ivelis has beautiful long naturally curly hair and when we're driving with the convertible top down her hair goes absolutely everywhere, even at relatively slow speeds. To keep all that hair somewhat under control, she wears a scarf in the manner that Grace Kelly did in her 1950s movies. So we named the car *Grace* and within a couple of months we got an appropriate vanity plate: 50 GRACE (GRACE alone wasn't available in Pennsylvania and we felt that adding a 50 would

The 50th Anniversary Corvette logo as seen on Grace's right front fender

June 2003: Grace & sister on the 50th Anniversary Corvette Caravan

nicely hint at *Grace*'s 50th Anniversary Edition status).

'Corvette Heaven'

Less than two months after picking up *Grace*, in late June 2003, we joined the 50th Anniversary Corvette Caravan. Over several days, we traveled from our house in Bryn Mawr, PA, met up with a few hundred Corvettes at the Carlisle Fairgrounds in Carlisle, PA, and drove down (with a stop at Bristol Motor Speedway) to the Corvette 50th Anniversary Celebration in Nashville, TN—a once in a lifetime gathering of around ten thousand Corvettes that Ivelis colorfully but fairly accurately described as 'Corvette Heaven'.

Test Runs

In the remaining two years before our second Route 66 trip, we drove some fairly long trips as 'test runs'. On Memorial Day weekend in 2004, we drove almost 2,000 miles in five days. After this, we felt reasonably 'shaken down' for a long trip, but both Ivelis and I were aware that there were still a lot of unknowns about taking an 18 day trip, which would be considerably longer than our previous Route 66 excursion had been five years before.

1 Leg One: Bryn Mawr, PA to Chicago, IL

Heading Out

We woke very early on Friday, April 1st, 2005 (our choice of this starting date gave some folks we know legitimate thought that this trip might be a fool's errand). One of the great inside jokes of "the Corvette lifestyle" is how many times this supposedly rather relaxed and glamorous life means that you are up at or before the crack of dawn. Since we had packed *Grace* as much as possible the evening before, we basically just woke up, showered, dressed, and headed out on the road, delayed by only a couple minutes as I took some pictures of the pristine car and futzed with our brand new iPod to CD-changer interface.

We pulled away from our house in Bryn Mawr at about 7:15 A.M. After traveling for a short period along a few local

Dawn, April 1st, 2005, Bryn Mawr, PA

arterial roads, we headed straight up the Northeast Extension of the Pennsylvania Turnpike, passing through Lansdale and Emmaus with a quick break for breakfast at a rather familiar rest stop along the way. Our overriding goal for day one was to get to the Pro Football Hall of Fame in Canton, Ohio

Grace beautifully detailed & ready to go—as clean as she would be the entire trip

to travel about 435 miles in one day.

It was a typical early spring day in the northeast United States, a bit chilly and grey but with signs showing up all around that winter was actually over. When we got near to Lake Harmony in the Pocono Mountains we turned west onto Interstate 80, making our first fuel stop at a British Petroleum in Harrisville and passing north of State College and through the towns of Du Bois, Grove City, and Hermitage on our way to Ohio and Canton.

well before it closed that same afternoon, so we didn't spend any time searching for any of Pennsylvania's scenic routes—we needed

Gilding The Lily?

Many Corvette owners substantially and significantly modify ('mod') their Corvettes. Ivelis isn't big on the idea of too many modifications (she calls it "gilding the lily")—she feels that Grace came pretty well equipped and configured from the factory. However, even she has been unable to resist a few:

Our first 'mod' was the horrible C5 Corvette cliche of aftermarket floormats, because the lovely but fragile 'shale' (actually light beige) colored ones with the 50th Anniversary logo that shipped with Grace are incapable of taking the kind of day to day pounding that floormats should.

Our first electronic 'mod' was a tiny little module called the Window Valet from a company called Top Down Technologies. This 'hack' adds remote control power windows and enhanced accessory power modes to the C5, all from the factory remote. It is especially useful for C5 convertible owners.

Our next significant 'mod' was fuel rail covers painted to match the exterior "Anniversary Red" color. The funny thing is that many non-Corvette folks think that these covers are stock (it makes sense the fuel rail covers would match the exterior), but Corvette people ooh and aah over them.

Another significant 'mod' (and the one that I believe Ivelis is proudest of) is our only true performance-related 'mod'—a Donaldson 'Blackwing' air filter assembly which adds about 10 horsepower.

Finally, when we're on a significant road trip with Grace like the subject of this book, we carry a 2-pound Halon fire extinguisher under the passenger seat in a fitted quick-disconnect brace.

Entering Ohio near Hubbard

After crossing the Pennsylvania/Ohio state border near Hubbard, we left Interstate 80 for Interstate 76 near Lordstown and headed past Niles and toward Akron. We turned south in Akron (home of Goodyear, long-time maker of the Corvette's performance tires) and headed south along Interstate 77 toward the Pro Football Hall of Fame in Canton.

Though we had driven past the Pro Football Hall of Fame in Canton several times, we had never actually visited it. Ivelis

Ivelis in front of the Pro Football Hall of Fame in Canton, OH

and I are both serious (almost fanatical) pro football fans, so we definitely weren't going to miss the Hall of Fame this time around. After taking a couple of pictures of the exterior of the building, we purchased our thirteen dollar tickets and eagerly headed in to see the exhibits.

For us, the Pro Football Hall of Fame was an impressive and worthwhile museum. The first thing the prospective visitor should know is that it is much bigger on the inside than it looks to be from the outside. The exhibits are well-designed and make a serious attempt to be comprehensive, including several other professional football leagues beyond the National Football League itself (though the NFL provides most of the funding).

The Gameday Stadium rotating theater, which takes viewers through a typical season from training camp to the Super Bowl, is also very interesting, though it wasn't as spectacular as we had been lead to believe by several friends. Finally, the newly updated Hall of Fame Gallery exudes class with its very simplicity, listing just the names, positions, teams, and relevant years with the busts—though you can call up vast amounts of amplifying information (including statistics and video footage) from the interactive consoles that sit in the middle of the room.

Busts in the Hall of Fame Gallery at the Pro Football Hall of Fame in Canton, OH

After purchasing a replica jersey and a ball cap at the Hall of Fame store, we left the building, drove about five miles north, and checked in for the night at the Best Western North Canton. As we headed out to dinner, we purchased two small umbrellas (I had unaccountably left our standard travel umbrellas back home) and some personal items at the local Giant supermarket.

We ate that night at a LongHorn Steakhouse near our Best Western. Af-

Where To Stay?

On this particular trip, our default place to stay when we were not in a large city was Best Western, because of what we saw as their general reliability, reasonable degree of comfort, and decent workout facilities. We viewed this choice as a sign that we are definitely moving up—on our first Route 66 trip in 2000 our default place to stay was Motel 6! In general, we were pleased with the Best Westerns we stayed at; we continue to consider them in small towns where we don't have any specific preference and they are relatively Corvette-friendly, usuallly having decent-sized parking lots with good lighting and visibility.

ter having a very good experience at the LongHorn (especially considering that it is one of those somewhat generic mid-price chains), we had to convince their highly customer service oriented managers that it wasn't worth their effort to make us come back (I thought their efforts would be better spent on folks who had better prospects for a quick return). I think we were both very happy to be on the road after so much planning and build-up, and so we had a relaxing dinner and a good night's sleep in North Canton.

Grace Sees Snow

The next morning we woke up to cold steady rain (at least we got to use our brand new umbrellas). As we started north from North Canton along Interstate 77, we ran into a condition we had definitely not

yet experienced in *Grace*—snow!

Snow is a problem in our generation of Corvette for two reasons: the vehicle design and the tires. The vehicle design issue is that the gorgeous, highly aerodynamic nose is so low that it effectively becomes a stunningly inefficient snowplow when the snow starts to pile up. The tires issue is that the standard Goodyear Eagle F1 GS Extended Mobility tires for C5 Corvettes are high performance summer tires with a rating of 2 out of 10 in the snow (and those tires were what we were driving on). As it continued to snow lightly, we traveled gingerly and unusually slowly past Akron, Elyria, Toledo (birthplace of NASA flight director Eugene "Gene" Kranz—"Failure is not an option!"), and Maumee along Interstate 80, stopping at a Sunoco in West Unity for fuel.

Luckily, the temperature never dropped below 30 degrees and the snow never really came down that hard or stuck that much. As we left Ohio for Indiana on Interstate 80, the snow began to thin out and then turned back to rain.

As we drove along Interstate 80 in Indiana we saw something we had never seen before in any of our travels in any car—a series of sensors and warning lights that attempt to warn drivers of deer or other large animals entering the roadway. I don't know how well the system works—and some quick background research seems to show that the jury is still out—but we certainly slowed down quickly when we saw one of the warning lights blinking!

Interesting sign & system near Orland, IN

During the next 100 miles further along the interstate, the weather cleared and the sun began to come out. Making relatively good time, we continued to progress swiftly along the combined Interstate 80 and Interstate 90, passing through Elkhart, South Bend (Notre Dame's famous gold dome was easily seen in the distance), Portage, Gary, and Hammond (home of the original Doublemint twins), on our way to Chicago.

For me, the marker that we have almost reached Chicago is always the toll plaza for the Chicago Skyway, with its distinctive art deco lettering—a reminder that it was completed in 1958. These last eight miles along the Skyway into Chicago almost give the feeling of flying over the outskirts of the city before diving down into the famous Chicago Loop.

Entering the Chicago Skyway from the Indiana Toll Road near Whiting, IN

In the early afternoon we pulled up to one of our favorite hotels, the Chicago Hilton. Chicago is home to many great hotels such as the Drake and the Fairmont, but the Hilton, a huge hotel on Michigan Avenue with spectacular views of the lake shore, remains our personal favorite. This particular Hilton was the largest hotel in the world when it was completed in 1927 and its public spaces are stunning (the rooms aren't too bad either).

As we were unloading the Corvette at the hotel driveway on Balbo Drive, I dropped my digital SLR. I had made the classic mistake so many of us are familiar

View of the Chicago Hilton in Chicago, IL from Lake Michigan

with—given the choice of two objects to drop, we will always drop the more expensive object. So instead of dropping a half-full plastic water bottle, I dropped my wonderful Nikon D70 about four feet, lens first onto concrete.

Not a good start, I thought, wondering at that moment if I was cursed for good cameras and long road trips (on our first Route 66 trip I had failed to check for the presence of film in our analog SLR until we got all the way to St. Louis). With this problem sitting in the back of my mind, I walked up to the reservation desk and began the process of checking in to the hotel.

Advantages Of A Big City

While we waited for our room to free up, I looked at the camera in the immense lobby of the Hilton. Taking a significant risk (please don't try this at home!), I turned the camera on. My D70 happily powered up and displayed its configuration and status correctly—I was experiencing one of the reasons folks so loyally buy Nikons. So far, so good—but the zoom lens was making ugly crunching sounds. I tried to take the lens cap off, but it was wedged into the ultraviolet (UV) filter. When I finally pried the lens cap off, a shattered UV filter came into view. Fine, I thought, I'll just replace the UV filter and I'll be good to go. Except the rather expensive UV filter would not unscrew from the quite expensive lens …

Feeling all to much like a typical clueless and helpless tourist, I went in near desperation to the Hilton's concierge desk, asking where the closest camera shop was. With a look that said that she was about to make me very happy (and get a nice tip), the concierge told me that the best camera shop in Chicago was four blocks away, on Wabash Avenue.

The wondrous Nikon D70, in an undamged state

As soon as we got situated in our room, I quickly walked over to the camera store the concierge had directed me to. Central Camera was as the Hilton's concierge had advertised; it is the kind of camera shop that only big cities still have (they've been in business since 1899). It's a long, thin, and somewhat dark store with every possible kind of photographic equipment stacked to the rafters and folks that actually know what they are talking about. They quickly pointed me back to the repair area when I told them what I needed.

The young lady in the repair area at Central Camera attempted several fixes and then sent me several blocks further north along Wabash Avenue to Chicago Camera Specialists, a tiny little camera repair shop located in a complex of jewelry stores. The owner of the repair shop worked on the lens assembly for about half an hour with no success (based on the other cameras I saw in his shop, my D70 was the cheapest camera he had worked on in quite a while). He explained that what had happened was that (under extreme duress) the UV filter had mass bonded itself to the screw threads on the lens. So, though the lens was working and only had a few scratches, it was time to get another lens, at least until I could get the distressed lens back to Nikon.

I went back to Central Camera, this time with a modified goal: buying a new zoom lens. I had been using the very good Nikkor 18-70 zoom lens that was bundled with the camera, but because it was a bundled lens a simple replacement was not available. I ended up settling on a really snazzy Nikkor 24-120 zoom lens with vibration reduction. Almost all of the rest of the pictures in this book were taken with this new lens, including some quick test photos of the monuments in Chicago's Grant Park.

A monument in Grant Park in Chicago, IL—the first picture taken with the new lens

In the end I was really lucky, considering the situation I had managed to get myself into. It was early Saturday afternoon, so stores were still open. Also, we were in a major metropolitan area with a capable and professional camera shop. Finally, we were within walking distance of one of those shops. When Ivelis saw the fancy new zoom lens and the considerable bill that came with it, she told me that it was my anniversary present!

After finally calming down from this (sort-of) emergency, I did take time to appreciate our excellent accommodations at the Chicago Hilton. This Hilton is really nice no matter where you are staying, but we were on the 'Executive Floor' and everything was just a bit nicer—a comfortable lounge and a very nice room.

It seems that Ivelis and I are on a sort of survey of 'touristy' Chicago food experiences. The first time we were in Chicago together we ate at Morton's of Chicago, so we had already done the Chicago steakhouse thing. This time around we were looking for the Chicago deep dish pizza experience, so we ate dinner at Pizzeria Due, which is on Wabash Avenue and is across the street from the original, tiny, and still incredibly crowded Pizzeria Uno (we stopped there but decided we didn't want to wait several hours to be seated). Even Due's was quite crowded (it was a Saturday night, after all) but we were perfectly happy to sit and eat at their bar. The Chicago deep dish pizza was as good as we expected, though we didn't notice a huge difference between what was available there and what you can get at any decent chain Uno's.

After a filling dinner, we took a taxi back to the hotel and had a few excellent drinks together at the very nice bar in the hotel lobby, the same bar we had enjoyed so much the first time we stayed at the Hilton five years before.

Statistics

Travel time for Leg 1, Bryn Mawr to Chicago: **2 days**

Miles traveled on this leg: **839 miles**

Total travel time: **2 days**

Total miles traveled: **839 miles**

Miles from home at end of this leg (shortest reasonable route): **745 miles**

2 Leg Two, Part I: Chicago, IL to Tucumcari, NM on Route 66

Picking Up Route 66

We drove slowly away from the Chicago Hilton at about 8:30 on a Sunday morning, narrowly avoiding getting stuck inside the route of a large 8K run that was about to start on the Lake Michigan shore line. We picked up the eastern starting point of Route 66 at the corner of Michigan Avenue and Adams Street and headed almost due west until we got to Ogden Avenue, at which point we angled left and headed southwest through the Chicago suburb of Cicero, probably best known for being Al Capone's (extremely illegal) base of operations in the 1920s.

After passing through Cicero and Joliet (birthplace of football player Mike Alstott), the next significant town on Route 66 is Wilmington. In the outskirts of Wilmington we passed directly to the left of what I think was our first example of notable Route 66 kitsch—the early 1960s Launching Pad Drive-In with its 28 foot tall 'Gemini Giant,' a green astronaut holding an oft-replaced rocket.

The Launching Pad Drive-In with its 'Gemini Giant' in Wilmington, IL

7

A view down Route 66 in Illinois—that's Interstate 55 to the right

A Millenium Yellow Corvette convertible on Route 66

Shortly after we drove through Wilmington, we got what I saw as our first 'real' Route 66 road feel as we traveled alongside Interstate 55. The long-unused telephone poles extend off toward the horizon, with some of the wires still attached, as if reactivating all those ancient cloth-covered copper lines is just a couple of switches and some light maintenance away. Despite being on the two lane highway instead of the four lane interstate, we made almost as good time as the folks on the boring 'superslab', only slowing down as we passed through small towns every several miles: Gardner, Dwight, Odell, Pontiac, …

Millennium Yellow Makes An Appearance

At three days into our road trip, we saw what was (somewhat unbelievably) our first other Corvette of the entire vacation while we were having a quick breakfast at the McDonalds in Chenoa. The other Corvette was a Millennium Yellow C5 convertible (Ivelis calls Millennium Yellow 'arrest-me yellow'—we think it's for people who think that bright red is just too restrained for a Corvette). I chatted for a short while with the owner, who had done portions of Route 66 in his convertible, but never the whole thing. He wished us luck on our trip, with perhaps just a little tinge of envy.

After our breakfast in Chenoa, we returned to Route 66 and headed through Lexington, Towanda, Normal, Bloomington (once the home and still the namesake of one of the biggest of all Corvette shows, Bloomington Gold), Shirley, Funks Grove (where you can get 'maple sirup'), McLean, Lawndale, Lincoln (actually named for Abraham Lincoln *before* he became president), Broadwell, and Elkhart, enjoying the weather as it got steadily warmer. At some point in the early afternoon we realized that we needed to move a bit faster if we were going to make it to St. Louis on schedule. So, after following Route 66 through the center of Springfield, we got on Interstate 55, passed through Litchfield, Mount Olive, and Collinsville (said to be the horseradish capital of the world), and headed across the Poplar Street bridge into St. Louis and Missouri.

Journey To The Top

We arrived in downtown St. Louis on a true 'Chamber of Commerce' day—it was absolutely and somewhat unexpectedly beautiful for early April: sunny and about 70 degrees. After rushing to the Jefferson National Expansion Memorial Park to make it in time for our 3:00 P.M. reservation for a tour up to the top of the Gateway Arch, we discovered that the tours were significantly backed up because the NCAA Men's Final Four basketball tournament was in town (a conflict I had somehow failed to note in

Children gather around a statue of Abraham Lincoln in Springfield, IL

my travel planning). However, it did turn out to have been a really good idea to have made reservations on-line—as soon as we

Looking almost straight down from the Gateway Arch in St. Louis, MO

got through the security checkpoint, we were able to get right in line for the tram to the top instead of waiting in yet another long line to buy tickets.

While we were waiting for the tram cars to arrive, we took a look at some of the historical exhibits about the Gateway Arch's construction. The impression I got is that the 630-foot tall Arch's getting built at all was a rather close-run thing—the early 1960s was not a time in United States history that we were building a lot of monuments and St. Louis was not an especially obvious place to take on this kind of project. I really admire Eero Saarinen's architecture—he designed many other well-known buildings such as the gorgeous TWA terminal at John F. Kennedy International Airport in New York City and the stunning (and huge) General Motors Technical Center in Warren, Michigan. I also found the technical details involved in the construction process (such as the materials used) to be very interesting.

When the eight tram cars came grinding slowly down to their stops, we (and almost all the other passengers) had only one thought: the cars are tiny, especially considering the steady expansion of the average size and girth of the American population. The designers managed to fit five seats into each tram car and it is quite tight—probably more than a little claustrophobic for some people. However, the ride to the top only takes only about four minutes, and the absolutely spectacular view when you get there is certainly worth it. I was able to take many pictures from the top, some of which came out very well, especially considering I was still learning how to use my new telephoto lens!

Looking across & down from the Gateway Arch into St. Louis, MO during the 2005 NCAA Final Four weekend

Stylish shot of the Gateway Arch from underneath in St. Louis, MO

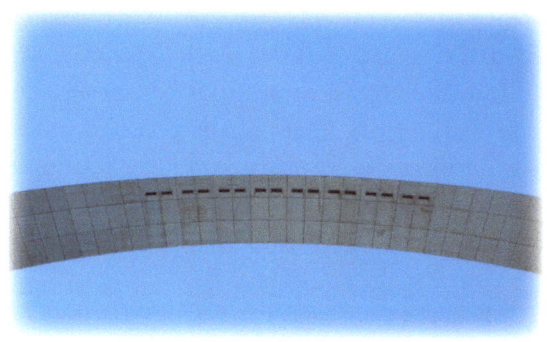

Close-up of the observation windows at the top of the Gateway Arch in St. Louis, MO

We took the tram back down to the bottom of the Arch—the ride down (aided by gravity) takes only about three minutes. In the ground underneath the Arch are an impressively large set of attractions, but we just grabbed a bottled water to share between the two of us and went back outside to take some more pictures of the Gateway Arch from the outside. The Arch is a great subject for an amateur photographer—it has many interesting and challenging angles and reflections, especially on a beautiful day like the one we experienced.

After I had finished taking pictures, we left the Jefferson National Expansion Memorial Park and headed toward the center of town to see what was going on with the Final Four-related activities. We sampled some of the food and music in Kiener Plaza for a little while. When we were finished, Ivelis had me take one last set of pictures of the Gateway Arch from the steps of the Historical Old Courthouse before we got on the road again.

One last view of the Gateway Arch, seen from the Historical Old Courthouse in St. Louis, MO

We drove out from the center of St. Louis into the suburbs with the convertible top down (getting some of our return on that extra convertible investment). On the way out, we passed the Bevo Mill restaurant, which is quite distinctive because it is topped by a windmill. The building itself was built by August Busch (of Anheuser-Busch fame) in the 1910s as a competitive beer-selling alternative to the saloons of the time, as those saloons sold only hard liquor. In the 1980s, it was restored to its original finery with Anheuser-Bush funding.

Since we were staying at the Best Western in Kirkwood, we had dinner at the Chili's all too conveniently located adjoining the Best Western—you don't even have to exit the building to get from your room to the restaurant. Ivelis enthusiastically sampled several of their 'Presidente Margaritas' and we shared views of our impressions on our first day of traveling Route 66 for the

The Gateway Arch silhouetted against the sun in St. Louis, MO

Windmill-topped restaurant in the St. Louis suburb of Bevo, MO

A Z06 follows us west of Springfield, MO

second time around, before turning in for the night.

The next day, we got up early in the morning (trying to beat the Monday morning rush hour around the city) and left the St. Louis suburbs, heading west-south-west on Interstate 44. We continued to enjoy absolutely wonderful weather for early April in the mid-west and had the convertible top down almost all of the day. In Eureka, we got off the interstate and stopped for a short while at the local Route 66 park. Afterwards, we traveled on Route 66 until we reached Saint Clair; the first but not the last town we would drive through on Route 66 that was named after a railroad engineer. Then it was back (mostly) on the interstate—I was mindful that we needed to get to Claremore, Oklahoma by the end of the day. We did, however, leave the interstate whenever things looked especially interesting, as they did in Cuba, St. James, Rolla, Lebanon, and St. Robert/Waynesville.

While Ivelis was driving in Halftown (just west of Springfield) we picked up a very sharp-looking black C5 Z06, who followed us for several miles before waving and turning off. I, of course, just had to get the camera out quickly and take a couple pictures of that Z06 … it's the Corvette way.

From Halftown, we headed mostly due west toward Kansas. After about 45 miles on the Interstate, we rejoined Route 66 in Duenweg and headed through Duquense and Joplin to the border.

A Short Excursion In Kansas

The shortest portion of Route 66 is in Kansas, which has only about 13 out of the 2,448 miles of the total route, or about one half of one percent of the sum distance involved in traveling John Steinbeck's 'Mother Road'. Kansas does seem to have a lot of attractive and specific Route 66 signage, almost certainly more per mile than any other state. We saw much of this

Route 66 makes a clearly-marked left turn in Kansas

A better photo from the 2000 trip: that's Ivelis in our Chrysler 300M barely visible aboard the lovely March Rainbow Arch Bridge near Riverton, KA

signage as we passed through the towns of Galena and Lowell on a what was a beautiful spring day.

Kansas is also home to the only remaining March Rainbow Arch Bridge on Route 66, which crosses Brush Creek near Riverton. This gorgeous bridge was saved from demolition in the early 1990s by the relentless efforts of the Kansas Route 66 Association.

Regrettably, our only actual stop in Kansas was for a quick but relatively late lunch at a quiet McDonalds along Route 69 in Baxter Springs. Baxter Springs, which is about half a mile north of the Oklahoma border, was the site of a Civil War battle or massacre, depending on your Union or Confederate viewpoint. It also features a general store that was robbed not once, but twice by Bonnie Parker and Clyde Barrow (the famous Bonnie and Clyde) in the space of about a month in 1933.

Oklahoma has the greatest amount of remaining Route 66 miles and the state's pride in this fact is obvious in many places. We entered Oklahoma about five miles from Quapaw and drove toward Claremore along Route 66, passing through Commerce, the childhood home of baseball great Mickey

Classic Arby's sign in Miami, OK

The beautifully restored Coleman Theatre in Miami, OK

Mantle. Next was Miami, with its stately, gorgeous, and beautifully restored Coleman Theatre, built in 1929. This restoration includes the original Wurlitzer organ that was installed when the theatre was built.

Heading along Route 66 somewhere in northeastern Oklahoma

After continuing on Route 66 through the tiny town of Narcissa, we rejoined Interstate 44 in Afton for about ten miles before returning to Route 66 in Vinita (the second oldest town in Oklahoma, established in 1871). For the last few miles of this day's journey, we traveled through Chelsea (the site of Oklahoma's first oil well in 1889) and Foyil before arriving in Claremore in the middle of the afternoon.

In Claremore, we stayed at the Will Rogers Inn. As Will Rogers himself said, he was born "halfway between Claremore and Oologah before there was a town at either place" in 1879 and Will's name is on just about everything in town. Our room, though quite well maintained, definitely had some touches from another era. In particular, our room's plastic (Bakelite, perhaps) and metal light and heat switches showed significant age and character.

Dated switches in our room in Claremore, OK

This particular evening was the first time we did our laundry on this trip, with Ivelis aggressively staking out the single available washer and dryer while I foraged successfully for packages of laundry detergent and bleach. All went as expected, making us a bit more confident in our planning of this part of the trip.

For dinner in Claremore that night,

The view northeast along Route 66 from our Best Western in Claremore, OK

we took a decidedly non-glamorous approach as there didn't seem to be very many choices within walking distance. We ate a decent and filling meal at the local greasy spoon and then headed to the nearly empty sports bar next door, where we talked quietly and drank a few domestic beers, taking in the many changes of the last several hundred miles.

A Whale, An Ark, & A Round Barn

Early the next morning we headed out of Claremore down Route 66. As Route 66 neophytes in 2000, we had driven by—but not stopped at—one of the most famous and distinctive of the Route 66 landmarks, the blue whale of Catoosa. This time around, we were absolutely *not* going to miss this stop! We drove around a slight bend in the road and there the large whale was, in all its, well, blueness.

I took many exterior and interior pictures of this 80-foot long blue whale,

A view from on board the blue whale in Catoosa, OK

Packing & Laundry

Packing our particular 'droptop' Corvette wasn't nearly as hard as it would have been with almost any other Corvette convertible ever made—

Grace's trunk, packed full & ready to go

there's significantly more room in the trunk of a C5 convertible than in any Corvette convertible made since the last of the C1 convertibles in 1962. There is, however, a lot less room than we had in our Chrysler 300M that we last traveled across the nation in (and, of course, there's no back seat in any Corvette). With the top down and a foam divider in (both to protect the top and keep the road noise down) there is probably about 11 cubic feet of trunk space available.

We packed fairly lightly, but flexibly, bringing a set each of workout clothes and dressy clothes in addition to our standard shirts and slacks. We planned for a lot of layering when it got cold and decided that we would do the laundry three times during the trip, or about every four to five days. In the end, all this planning worked out—we never felt truly short of clothing and we never ran out of trunk space, despite picking up some souvenirs along the way.

built out of concrete in the early 1970s by Hugh Davis for his wife Zelta as a surprise anniversary present—as someone who is constantly trying to come up with great, exciting, or unusual gifts for Ivelis, I have to wonder how he topped that gift the following year!

The blue whale is actually in much better shape than it was five years ago; an enterprising group of local citizens have repainted and otherwise refurbished the whale, which (amazingly) does not seem to have a name, official or otherwise.

On the same site as the blue whale there's also a cleverly named A.R.K. (Animal Reptile Kingdom) edifice, which housed

Welis aboard the famous and fabulous blue whale of Catoosa, OK

The decrepit A.R.K. (Animal Reptile Kingdom) in Catoosa, OK

various reptiles, including alligators, during the 1970s and 1980s. The wooden A.R.K. is now rotting away and fenced off for safety reasons, but remains an interesting and imposing sight.

After Catoosa (which is also a fairly significant port), we took Interstate 44 through Tulsa and Sapulpa, exiting again onto Route 66 near Kellyville and passing through Depew, Stroud, Davenport, Chandler, and Warwick. A couple of hours later that morning, we stopped for an excellent breakfast at a small, family-style diner in mid Oklahoma. The local folks at the diner warned us that bad weather was coming, with high winds and possibly hail (we must have exuded 'tourist' that morning). Soon, it began to look like they were right—the winds really started to pick up as we traveled across Oklahoma.

As we moved on, we stopped at the only round barn on Route 66, which is in Arcadia, just a bit to the northeast of Oklahoma City. In 2000, the barn (which was built in 1898) was not open when we drove through, but this time around it was. We talked to a very interesting gentleman inside the barn who had a fairly encyclopedic knowledge (along with more than a few reference books) of round barns in the United

Parked oh so stylishly outside the round barn in Arcadia, OK

States and Canada. I, of course, could not resist the chance to buy yet another set of descriptive Route 66 maps, these ones by Jerry McClanahan and Jim Ross (Jim Ross lives in Arcadia).

We drove through Oklahoma City on Interstate 44, exiting back onto Route 66 near Bethany and passing through Yukon (childhood home of country singer Garth Brooks) and El Reno before joining Interstate 40 for the first time. In Weatherford, we got off the interstate and drove by the Thomas Stafford Air and Space Museum, named after Apollo 10's mission commander (we'll make sure to stop there next time—the museum includes an F-86 Sabre jet fighter from the Korean War along with some other interesting aircraft and exhibits).

F104 Starfighter on display outside the Thomas Stafford Air & Space Museum in Weatherford, OK

More Treasures Along The Route

A little further down the road in Clinton, we visited our favorite of the several (every state seems to have one) Route 66 museums. This is another attraction that we had visited on our first Route 66 trip in 2000 (I actually still have a t-shirt from that first visit which I wore in honor of my visit this time around).

Entering El Reno, OK

17

A chunk of original road concrete at the Oklahoma Route 66 Museum in Clinton

Grace outside the Oklahoma Route 66 Museum in Clinton

The Oklahoma Route 66 Museum follows the history of Route 66 over the decades, with interesting and informative displays that show both the development and the fading away of 'The Mother Road', along with its potential futures. I believe that the museum succeeds in being both educational and amusing, something not too many museums that I have visited achieve. We did drop almost a hundred dollars in the gift shop, showing the considerable effectiveness of the museum's soft sell.

Stylish neon shot inside the Oklahoma Route 66 Museum in Clinton

A Microbus with a split personality inside the Oklahoma Route 66 Museum in Clinton

After our enjoyable time at the museum in Clinton, we returned to Interstate 40 and passed through Canute, Elk City, and Sayre on our way to Texas.

The main goal for our trip through Texas along Route 66 was to visit the famous (and famously strange) Cadillac Ranch, now in its new location, moved two miles further outside of Amarillo in 1997. The Cadillac Ranch was another Route 66 landmark we had driven by but not stopped to visit in 2000.

On our way across the Texas panhandle, we passed the leaning water tower in Groom, deliberately built at an angle by the Britten family as an advertisement for their truck stop. The truck stop is long gone (it burned down), but the water tower remains, still leaning at the same angle and still getting the originally intended stares and questions from curious travelers.

Deliberately leaning water tower advertises a long gone truck stop in Grimm, TX

As we drove though Texas, the winds continued to get stronger and the skies more threatening. "What happens if it hails?," I thought, starting to look for convenient overpasses to park under if the hail began.

The Cadillac Ranch

The Cadillac Ranch was created from ten old and mostly decrepit Cadillacs in 1974 by a set of artists called Ant Farm commissioned by Stanley Marsh 3 (he considers 'III' to be pretentious—I think he could always just drop the '3'). One of the legends about the Cadillac Ranch that I read when young is that it was at least partially inspired by a book on automobile styling, but I have not been able to confirm this. As a visitor to this very public piece of art, one is encouraged to visit the Cadillacs up close on the ranch (as long as you don't let the cows out) and graffiti is permitted if one is so inclined—they repaint the cars every couple of years to give the next round of folks a fresh base to work from.

By the time we got to the Cadillac Ranch, it was so windy that the cows were huddled for protection under those ten old Cadillacs. We climbed out of our nice warm car into the stiff winds, opened the

Ivelis poses with one of the grafitti-covered Cadillacs at the Cadillac Ranch in Amarillo, TX

Long shot of the Cadillac Ranch outside of Amarillo, TX

Cows seek shelter from stiff, chilly winds at the Cadillac Ranch in Amarillo, TX

gate, and walked into the field. When we got close to the Cadillacs, the cows moved, but with looks of resigned annoyance—you could almost hear them mooing "Tourist!". We took a couple of pictures and dashed back across the field to our waiting Corvette.

We had planned to stop in Vega, Texas, for the night. Vega looked fairly large on the computerized map in Microsoft's Streets & Trips software. It wasn't—it looked like the (bad) movie cliche of the western ghost town when we actually arrived, with tumbleweeds flying across the main intersection in town as the single stoplight blinked red and swayed in the gusts of wind. The only person we saw in the entire town of about 900 was the woman at the Vega Best Western who very kindly helped us change our reservations from Vega to Tucumcari.

'Tucumcari Tonite'

As we left Texas for New Mexico along Interstate 40, the brooding skies we had been seeing for the last few hundred miles began to yield, along with at least some of the strong wind. The contrast between the nice and nasty weather was sudden and glorious.

We pulled into Tucumcari that night with a huge sigh of relief and one very dirty *Grace*. We had travelled over 500 fairly hard miles that day, with the last 80 from Vega to Tucumcari being completely unexpected.

Since we had changed our reservations from the Vega Best Western, we ended up staying at one of the two Best Westerns in Tucumcari, instead of one of the extremely distinctive and legendary in-

Dark skies yield to bright skies as we leave Texas

Grace parked in Tucumcari, NM, not exactly looking her best

dependent motels, such as the Blue Swallow (in fact, we were lucky to get into the Best Western with so little warning—it was completely full by the time I had finished my check-in process).

Tucumcari is one of those places that Route 66 made huge—'Tucumcari Tonite!' is still the slogan on the billboards, which used to advertise '2,000 motel rooms', but now list 1,200. In spite of this downsizing, my impression was that the folks in Tucumcari are definitely making a go of it—it's still a fairly big town, with a lot going on. Tucumcari is also where the main action in the Clint Eastwood movie *For A Few Dollars More* is set, though of course this 'spaghetti western' was actually shot in Spain.

Battered Pony Soldier sign, along with ...

Mural in Tucumcari, NM

... the Palomino sign and the ...

More than a little exhausted and stressed out, we stumbled over for dinner at K-Bobs, a large regional chain with a restaurant located immediately adjacent to the Best Western. Afterward, we walked around Tucumcari a little bit and Ivelis had an ice cream before we headed back to our room at the Best Western for some much-needed sleep.

Statistics

Travel time for Leg 2, Part I, Chicago to Tucumcari: **3 days**
Miles traveled on this leg: **1,231 miles**
Total travel time: **5 days**
Total miles traveled: **2,070 miles**
Miles from home at end of this leg (shortest reasonable route): **1,722 miles**

... Blue Swallow sign, all in Tucumcari, NM

3 Leg Two, Part II: Tucumcari, NM to Santa Monica, CA on Route 66

Santa Fe: 'The City Different'

The next morning, we filled up *Grace*'s gas tank and our stomachs in Tucumcari and headed west along Interstate 40, traveling through Newkirk, Cuervo, and Santa Rosa (site of the train scene in the film version of *The Grapes Of Wrath*). At Vegas Junction, we turned northwest along Route 84 through sparse terrain, passing through Dilla before joining Interstate 25. From Ojitos Fritos, we traveled on Interstate 25 through Tecolote, Blanchard, San Ysidro (a village settled in 1699), and Rowe before getting off the interstate for a little while in Pecos and Glorieta.

We got back on Interstate 25 (there didn't seem to be many other options) and continued through Glorieta Pass, scene of another Civil War battle (we seem to have been unintentionally doing somewhat of a battlefield tour) in 1862. After making an early and wrong turn off the interstate (because I hadn't given Ivelis a clear description of where we were going), we correctly exited onto Route 466 and headed north into downtown Santa Fe.

Along Route 84, near Dilla, NM

23

We arrived in Old Santa Fe at around noon on a gorgeous day—though it always seems to be gorgeous in Santa Fe. We are big fans of the easily walkable center of Santa Fe, with it's Spanish Pueblo Revival and Spanish Territorial architecture, wonderful restaurants, and enticing shops. I believe it is truly 'The City Different.'

The Palace of Governers in old Santa Fe, NM

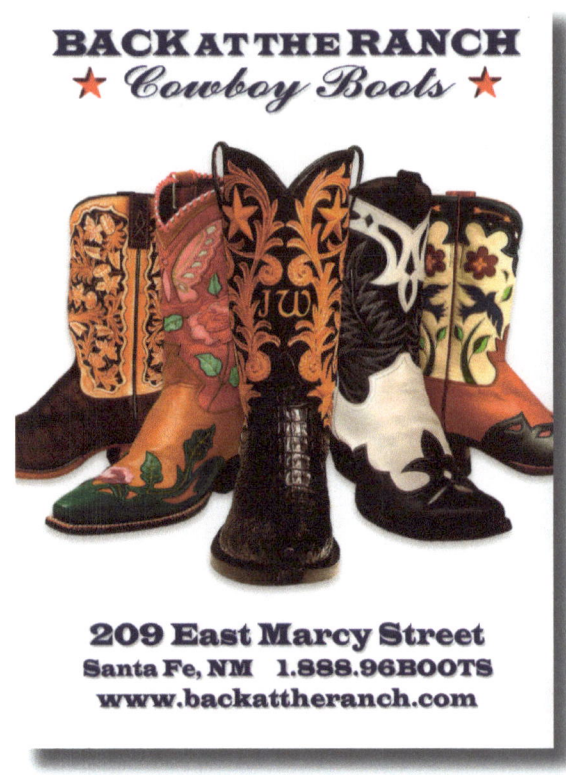

The card that got us to Back at the Ranch in Santa Fe, NM

In Santa Fe, we stayed at the superlative Eldorado Hotel, which I think is probably the best hotel in Santa Fe and probably the best hotel we stayed on our entire trip. Demonstrating a useful and profitable knowledge of what might be important to Corvette owners, the parking attendants at the Eldorado offered me a $20 basic overnight car wash. I swiftly took them up on it—*Grace* was still showing the sad effects of the wind and dust in Texas.

Ivelis Gets Her Boots

Ivelis has always wanted a pair of fine, custom-made cowboy boots, so after taking care of some necessities and mailing some post cards, we marched over to Back at the Ranch on East Marcy Street in Old Santa Fe. This is an amazing store, with a vast selection of gorgeous, very well crafted cowboy boots made in places all over the southwest part of the United States.

I got the feeling that we required significantly less shmoozing than the usual customers they see—they offered us a choice of wine or beer, but we did not partake (Ivelis had a water). Despite the profusion of exotic styles, Ivelis fairly quickly decided on a simple but exquisite design, brown with an inlaid pattern and a pointed toe. We paid the considerable price and we walked happily back to the hotel.

The Geronimo Legend

When evening came, we headed out to dinner after having some very good drinks at our hotel's bar, the Eldorado Cafe. When we last traveled Route 66 in 2000, we ate lunch at Mark Miller's Coyote Cafe in Old Santa Fe at the suggestion of a friend and had a great experience. This time around, I made reservations to go back there for dinner, but we were arriving on Wednesday and the Coyote Cafe wasn't yet open for the season on weekdays. So I asked the woman I was talking to from the Coyote Cafe "Where do you go for a really nice dinner in Santa Fe if you can't go to the Coyote Cafe?" She said, "Geronimo" I then made reservations at Geronimo, sight unseen.

Geronimo was just far enough away from our hotel so as not to be easily walkable, so the folks at the Eldorado reserved us a cab. When we said we were going to Geronimo, the cabbie who picked us up said just enough admiring things about the restaurant to make us wonder whether he was on the payroll.

Geronimo is located in a 1756 adobe home on Canyon Road. The chef, Eric DiStefano, has created an absolutely spectacular restaurant within those old walls. We enjoyed ourselves to the fullest—great food, great drink, great service, and great ambiance. We'll definitely be back to eat at Geronimo the next time we're stopping in Santa Fe—one of our favorite cities in all the world.

A C5 Corvette coupe parked outside of the Geronimo Restaurant in Santa Fe, NM

"¡Pricessa De Puerto Rico Levantaste Y Bailé!"

We took another cab back to the Eldorado Hotel and headed down to the hotel bar for a nightcap. Back at the Eldorado Cafe, a very good Mexican guitarist and vocalist named Antonio Mendoza was playing to a small crowd. As we walked by (heading for the excellent bar) Ivelis greeted him in Spanish. A couple of songs later, Antonio challenged Ivelis (in Spanish) to dance (the English translation is "Puerto Rican princess, get up and dance!"), so, of course, she did—to wild applause that did not only come from her husband. Soon, the previously empty dance floor began to fill up.

After this unexpected excitement (though I've noticed that these things do seem to happen when I'm with Ivelis), we sat down and talked with another couple who were enjoying the music and the ambience. They mentioned that they had chanced upon Antonio Mendoza in several venues across the Southwest and he was always excellent.

Getting ready to check out; quite early in the morning inside the Eldorado Hotel in Santa Fe, NM

We got up even earlier than our usual early rising the next morning, with high hopes of beating at least some of the rush hour Santa Fe/Albuquerque traffic. More than a little bleary-eyed from the previous evening's festivities, we somewhat grudgingly checked out of our wonderful newish hotel in old Santa Fe in our newly-washed (and thus far more respectable looking) Corvette, leaving the center of the city and heading almost due south on Route 84 before rejoining Interstate 25 and heading southwest through Bernallilo, past Rio Rancho (home of Intel's Fab 11X—what may be the most advanced semiconductor plant in the world), and toward Albuquerque.

After making the correct turn (right, in this case—we did not impersonate a certain Warner Brothers cartoon character) at Albuquerque we headed west along Interstate 40 toward Arizona in reassuringly moderate traffic, picking up a tank of fuel and a good diner breakfast in Gallup shortly before crossing the state border some time in mid-morning.

Crossing from New Mexico into Arizona near Gallup, NM

Once we were in Arizona, we headed along Interstate 40 for about 40 miles through Chambers and to the Petrified Forest National Park—a major item on our list of attractions despite our having seen it before. We got off the interstate at exit 311, which dropped us right at the northern entrance to the park where we picked up a guide map at the visitor's center. After paying the small entry fee and affirming to a park ranger that we would not take petrified wood from the park (this is evidently, unfortunately, and more than a little painfully still a significant problem), we drove into the park itself.

Top Down In The Petrified Forest

We had driven through the Petrified Forest National Park once before in 2000 in our Chrysler sedan, but it was a completely different, far more visceral expe-

Beauty shot of Grace in the painted desert portion of the Petrified Forest National Park, AZ

rience driving through the park in an open car. Driving with the top down emphasizes

Unbelievable beauty in the painted desert portion of the Petrified Forest National Park, AZ

the stunning beauty and the wide openeness of the spaces and also adds some desert sounds to the experience.

The Petrified Forest was designated as a national monument in 1906 during Theodore Roosevelt's administration (the whole park including the painted desert potions became a national park in 1962). If one enters the park from the north, one begins with about 10 miles of the painted desert, with several spectacular overlooks.

There's an interesting stop about halfway through the park at a partially excavated ancient Ancestral Puebloan settlement called Puerco Pueblo, which was inhabited from about 1250 to 1400. In addition to the settlement itself, there are many petroglyphs (drawn by the original inhabitants and others) easily visible on the surrounding rocks.

After viewing the ruins and petroglyphs at Puerco Pueblo, we returned to our Corvette just as two lady tourists from the United Kingdom were finishing taking a set of pictures of themselves in front of it. Amused, we let them take a few more shots before we resumed our travels—one thing about owning any Corvette convertible is that you are never lonely!

After the settlement, there's what

Petroglyphs in the painted desert portion of the Petrified Forest National Park, AZ

Bright colors in the Petrified Forest National Park in Arizona

'Old Faithful' in the Petrified Forest National Park in Arizona

I consider the park's 'big finish'—several stops which feature large portions of the brightly colored petrified forests themselves. Ivelis and I both believe that all the parts of the Petrified Forest National Park are spectacular, just in different ways.

Rabbit Trading Post ("Here It Is!", say the signs) in Joseph City.

We jumped off the interstate and traveled along Route 66 through Winslow (of Eagles' lyric fame) and Flagstaff (a fairly large town that for some obscure reason is often mentioned in Tom Hanks' films).

Dinosaurs outside the Rainbow Rock Shop in Holbrook, AZ

Winslow, AZ—I did not stand on any corner

Green Dinosaurs In Holbrook

We exited the southern part of the park and drove northwest on Highway 180 toward the town of Holbrook. In Holbrook, a set of concrete green dinosaurs outside the Rainbow Rock Shop come up suddenly as one enters the center of town—another reason why one should *always* have one's camera ready on the road. A relatively small town, Holbrook was named after H.R. Holbrook, the first chief engineer of the Atlantic and Pacific Railroad, which passed through Holbrook.

From Holbrook, we headed almost due west along Interstate 40, passing the famous and still heavily advertised Jack

The next to come was Williams, which was (due to extended and extensive litigation) the final town to have its section of Route 66 bypassed by Interstate 40 in 1984. After Williams the next town of any size is Seligman, population about 450. We pulled over outside of the Roadkill Cafe in Seligman and prepared for a significnt chunk of fast top-down driving.

Route 66 Motel sign in Seligman, AZ

After Seligman, Route 66 splits significantly from Interstate 40, which has otherwise been ever-present since Oklahoma City except for where Route 66 goes through Santa Fe. At this point, Route 66 heads into significantly more mountainous and far more lonely country, first northwest toward Peach Springs and then southwest

Another better shot from 2000: a Jack Rabbit billboard outside of Joseph City, AZ

Preflight for serious top-down driving...

...Welis puts her scarf on outside the...

...Roadkill Cafe in Seligman, AZ

through Truxton.

This driving (about 100 miles that felt far too short to me) was wonderful and exhilarating in our Corvette, or, I think, any powerful sports car: fast, but interesting, with many sweeping curves—giving one the feeling of being where one's car is in its element.

Our drive that day finished in Kingman, one of the major transportation centers in Arizona. Kingman, founded in 1882, is a relatively small and attractive city with a significant amount of historical interest and a strong sense of its Route 66 heritage.

Mural painted (with an appropriate Corvette) by local artist Sandy Rusinko in Kingman, AZ

Celebrating Our Wedding Anniversary In Kingman, AZ

That night, which was the actual night of our tenth wedding anniversary (April 7th), we stayed at the Holiday Inn Express in Kingman. Someday, I'll manage to have us stay in some glamorous hotel or resort on our anniversary night while on one of our major road trips—so far, I'm 0 for 2, having placed us in small towns with

Somewhere between Seligman and Kingman in April 2000

One of many Route 66 markers on the road in Kingman, AZ

Getting Out & About

At almost every location we stayed on this trip (in fact, on any long road trip we have taken together) I tried to step out of the hotel or motel, walk around, and get a general feel for the neighborhood located around whatever our resting place for the night might be.

Aside from the obvious fitness-related plusses, this short to medium length walk often had significant positive payoffs. I was careful to make note of the location of essentials such as drug stores, post offices, and auto parts stores. I also found wonderful restaurants that we would never have seen mentioned in the local guidebooks, or even if we had seen them mentioned we would not have seen fit to consider—there's often no substitute for a visual inspection. Sometime, of course, Ivelis sent me out with specific needs, requests, queries, or requirements …

Exterior of Mr. D'z diner in Kingman, AZ

Sign on roof of Mr. D'z diner in Kingman, AZ

decent but not great accommodations and restricted dining options on both our fifth and tenth anniversaries. Ivelis has always been a good sport about this lack of timing skills demonstrated by the husband, but I'd like to do better.

Despite the notable lack of glamour, we ate a quiet, relaxed, and enjoyable dinner at a decent family restaurant (our personable waitress was from New Jersey) across the street from the Holiday Inn Express and turned in for the night not too long thereafter.

Breakfast At Mr. D'z

The next morning we packed up and drove down the street about a mile to Mr. D'z Route 66 Diner for breakfast. This beautiful old diner, once a gas station (Texaco, I believe) and currently resplendent in pink and blue, was one of Ivelis' essential stops on this second Route 66 tour (she had been asking about our chances of visiting it for approximately the previous 500 miles). The ambiance is wonderful, the service good, and the food is classic diner food, which we both have a *serious* weakness for. As expected, we greatly enjoyed our breakfast of sausage and eggs and hotcakes and home fries and …

One of the things that most amused Ivelis at Mr. D'z diner is that the Formica® at the diners counter had the exact same 'boomerang' pattern as our early 1960s kitchen countertop had at home. She had me take a couple of close-up pictures as proof.

Just across the street from the Mr.

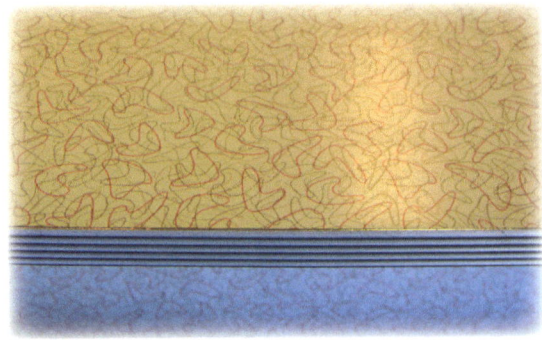

The 'boomerang' counter pattern at Mr. D'z in Kingman, AZ

D'z diner is a huge and historic Baldwin locomotive, number 3759, which traveled over two million miles for the Santa Fe

Huge Baldwin locomotive in Kingman, AZ

A sense of scale is essential out west; me on board the giant locomotive in Kingman, AZ

railroad in the 1920s, 1930s, 1940s, and 1950s, making its final run in February 1955. The locomotive, along with a large matching tender and a classic red caboose, dominates a small park right next to Route 66. After breakfast, we wandered over to the park, took some pictures with and of this huge old steam engine, and imagined it pulling all those fast passenger expresses and long freights over the years.

Negotiating The Twisties, Then & Now

Following our time at the diner and the locomotive, we headed southwest out of Kingman onto what I believe is the most mountainous, twistiest, and tightest portion of the entire Route 66—parts that the much newer Interstate 40 completely bypasses (it travels through much flatter country well to the south). The tight switchbacks (how many tens or hundreds of turns are there on this route?) go on for miles in rugged country, with sheer dropoffs often present.

One wonders how early travelers of this part of the route safely negotiated these daunting curves in their Ford Model Ts and Model As, with power nothing. Several sources state that travelers passing through often hired local drivers who were more familiar with the curves and drove up the hills in reverse to better utilize the primitive gravity-fed fuel systems of the day. As a stark warning for those who might not yet be paying attention, you could see some burnt out hulks of old cars and trucks at the bottom of a few of the gorges.

Though quite challenging to me (and perhaps a bit tense for Ivelis), this portion of Route 66 was some of the most interesting and notable driving of the entire trip, with *Grace's* 'trick' F55 magnetic ride

Rugged country approaching Oatman, AZ

suspension performing with all of the confidence-inspiring aplomb that those hard-working Chevrolet engineers had intended.

At approximately the midpoint of these twisties is Oatman, a tiny and old former gold mining town so completely out of the way that Clark Gable and Carol Lombard honeymooned in its single small hotel for an evening in 1939 after getting married at St. John's Methodist Church in Kingman. Oatman is also noted for the wild burros that roam its few streets—I think I may have driven even more carefully in the center of town than in the roads near it!

After spending some more time slowly negotiating the remaining twisties after Oatman, we headed through the small town of Topock and over the Colorado River into California.

We entered California near the city of Needles and took the opportunity to fill up our gas tank there—we remembered from our 2000 trip that gas stations were few and far between in the California desert, in addition to being very expensive. Needles, founded in 1883, was initially named "The Needles," after the sharp mountain peaks at the southerly end of the Mojave Valley. Heading through Needles in April was definitely more civilized than heading through it during July or August, when the temperature routinely hits 120 degrees in the early afternoon.

Old Route 66 In California

After our pause in Needles we headed into the Mojave Desert, passing through the tiny towns of Goffs, Essex (population 20), and Amboy (home of the well known but currently closed Roy's Motel and Cafe) along what the state of California calls the National Trails Highway.

Passing through tiny Oatman, AZ

In more of the serious twisties after leaving Oatman, AZ

A sign welcomes us to Needles & California

shape—more than once I wondered about *Grace's* glass reinforced plastic (GRP) bodywork and general mechanical health after hitting large chunks of disintegrating asphalt and concrete roadway at fairly high speed. Along this route, we drove by the abandoned Road Runner's Retreat in Chambless, probably best known for being the subject of a painting by Jerry McClanahan.

This portion of the trip was, if anything, more bleak and empty than the Arizona portion we had just passed through, in part because the roads are in far worse

The Road Runner's Retreat is no more: Chambless, CA

Amboy, CA; Roy's Motel and Cafe was closed, but it hadn't been so for that long ...

As we headed west, we ran into a large but strung-out group of motorcyclists heading east. I don't know who was more surprised to see whom: us, to see so much

What's Different About A Convertible

Purchasing a fabric-topped convertible instead of a hard-topped coupe most definitely involves commitment and some changes.

On the minus side, you give up two kinds of security. One, a convertible is much easier to break into (even the thickest, toughest canvas is easier to slash than steel, aluminum, or glass reinforced plastic). Two, it leaves you far more vulnerable in the event of a rollover; though the windshield frame is immensely strong (a C5 Corvette convertible can be statically balanced upside down on it) the primary risk in a convertible rollover is of being ejected from the passenger compartment. We always wear our seat belts and also have confidence that Grace's superb engine, handling, and brakes can minimize the chances of ever being in a rollover—what sports car drivers call 'active safety.'

However, you get considerable compensation for this lack of security. First, you get to hear nature—birds singing, babbling brooks, roaring rivers—and hearing things definitely makes you feel less isolated from your surroundings as you travel. Second, you interact with people on your route much more; folks yell complements, ask you where you are from, direct you to local landmarks, or just wave. Finally, there's just something special about a Corvette convertible on the open road—several different people looked at our car and exclaimed "Now that's the way to travel Route 66!"

A convertible is a different experience and somewhat more risky but we find those trade-offs completely worth it.

Long freight train rumbles through the Mojave Desert

Much of Route 66 remains fairly drivable, but there are some portions that are definitely not (at least not in a car with low ground clearance like our Corvette). We stopped and turned back to the interstate after running into wild flowers growing unmolested on the old road in California near Ludlow.

Flowers hint strongly that we should turn around, somewhere near Ludlow, CA

Though I knew in my head that we were in California, it really felt like we had truly arrived when we stopped at an interstate rest stop and parked next to a palm

Definitely in California!

riders so far out in the desert or them to see a still relatively pristine Corvette convertible, top down, 'hammer down.' We waved, of course—we wave to all motorcyclists, figuring that they share our same urge to experience active driving, instead of merely traveling from point A to point B.

Old Route 66 often followed and continues to follow the even older railroad tracks. One gets a sense of the amazing amount of cargo transport required to keep goods and services moving in the United States when you see extremely long diesel freight trains rumble by out west, often with three, four, or five large diesel locomotives straining to pull their immense and varied loads.

tree.

We left the desert and headed southwest toward San Bernadino, passing through Barstow, Helendale, and Oro Grande before joining Interstate 15 in Victorville. From Victorville on to the coast, the scenery and buildings begin to have that coastal built-up feel that we are familiar with on the east coast. As we headed out due west from San Bernadino to Santa Monica along Interstate 10, the highway continued to widen and the lanes continued to multiply at a fairly incredible rate—the endless profusion of Los Angeles roads and traffic never ceases to amaze me.

We also began to see cars and other vehicles that definitely seemed distinctively Californian in their weirdness. In particular, I vividly remember seeing a mid-1990s Infiniti j30t that had an almost new-age lowrider look about it, with very small whitewall tires extending out from the body—I managed to take a quick picture.

Heading for the Santa Monica Pier behind a BMW 2002—there's grit on our windshield from peices of the Mojave Desert

Pier on the coast of the Pacific Ocean. After missing the last exit and having to circle around through the hills of residential Santa Monica, we finally drove out onto the pier, parked, and stretched our legs.

Driving onto the old Santa Monica Pier in Santa Monica, CA

Distinctive Infiniti j30t, on Interstate 10 in Los Angeles, CA

We also began to see the expected classics and exotics—a 'Flair Bird' mid-1960s Ford Thunderbird, a late 1960s/early 1970s BMW 2002, and a fairly new Porsche 911 Turbo Convertible all passed us as we headed fairly slowly and deliberately toward Santa Monica—we were cognizant of our complete lack of knowledge about the local traffic patterns.

Ivelis and I had already decided that when we arrived in Santa Monica, we would head straight for the Santa Monica

The Santa Monica Pier was built in 1909 and some portions are really quite lovely. At the beginning of *The Sting*, Johnny Hooker (Robert Redford) finds Henry Gondorff (Paul Newman) operating a carousel in Chicago—that carousel is actually the one on the Santa Monica Pier.

Those high winds we had experienced in Texas seemed to have followed us—though it was a beautiful day, it was blowing so hard it actually took a bit of effort to walk out to the end of the pier.

It was a great feeling to have finished the Route 66 portion of the tour. In the pictures taken of me at this point, you can see a big smile, perhaps of relief, perhaps of happiness, maybe a combination—

View back down the Santa Monic Pier in Santa Monica, CA

A bit posed, but not that much (look at Welis' hair)—on the Santa Monica Pier in Santa Monica, CA

something you don't usually see in pictures of me.

Parked & extremely happy on the Santa Monica Pier in Santa Monica, CA

That night we stayed at The Huntley Hotel, a newly renovated (it was just in the process of re-opening) early 1960s hotel with extremely attractive and hi-tech (though somewhat small) rooms. For dinner, we walked to Houston's, a truly California style fusion of steakhouse and sushi restaurant on Wilshire Boulevard. After a few excellent Manhattens at the stylish bar, we sat in the 'cheap seats' (it was once again a Saturday night, and we didn't feel like waiting for a table) and had some very good sushi.

Leg two of our trip was complete—only two more legs and about 4,400 miles to go!

Statistics

Travel time for Leg 2, Part II, Tucumcari to Santa Monica: **3 days**
Miles traveled on this leg: **1,141 miles**
Total travel time: **8 days**
Total miles traveled: **3,211 miles**
Miles from home at the end of this leg (shortest reasonable route): **2,699 miles**

4 Leg Three: Santa Monica, CA to Seattle, WA

Meeting Up With Andy & Tamiza

On Saturday morning, we woke up and had breakfast at the restaurant at on the top floor of the The Huntley Hotel (where we were staying) with one of my Corvette friends and his lady.

Andy Bogus (I will freely admit that I didn't believe that was his real last name when I first met Andy) is one of my best friends on the Corvette Forum—he's helped me out many times with various technical information and general support, and he's just an all-around good guy. It was the first time either Ivelis or myself had met Tamiza and we vastly enjoyed her company. The four of us had a long and very relaxed breakfast, telling each other various Corvette and travel-related stories and enjoying the great view.

Andy & Tamiza join us for a fun, relaxing breakfast in Santa Monica, CA

After breakfast, we said goodbye to Andy and Tamiza, finished the rest of our packing, and left the hotel in Santa Monica. The plan for leg three of our trip was to follow the Pacific Coast Highway (California State Route 1) as much as possible through California, joining U.S. Highway 101 in Oregon, turning inland near Salem, passing through Portland and ending the leg in Seattle—about 1,500 miles.

Automotive Eye Candy

It was an absolutely gorgeous day, though just a little too chilly to comfortably travel with the top down. As seems to be normal for southern California on a Saturday morning, there was a fairly constant car show going on—a very handsome silver Aston Martin DB9 led us north out of Santa Monica.

This kind of automotive eye candy continued throughout the morning as we headed northwest up along the Pacific Coast Highway. In Malibu, we stopped for fuel just before noon at a Shell along the highway. One pump over from us was a fellow filling up his black Ferrari 250 GT Coupe as if there was nothing remotely abnormal about driving this late 1950s/early 1960s classic in busy California traffic. I was so stunned I failed to take any pictures!

A Ferrari 250 GT Coupe—but not the one we saw in Malibu…

We continued up the Pacific Coast Highway, driving past the Pacific Missile Test Center in Point Magu and through Oxnard, where we stopped at the local post office to get several post cards in the mail.

Along with the now expected fabulously rare and expensive vehicles, there were also what I call 'automobiles of unusual interest'—ones you don't see back on the east coast except as highly abused beaters or badly rusted wrecks or near-wrecks. I think this is one of the neatest things about the combination of the California car culture and the generally good weather in the

Sharp late 70s/early 80s El Camino (that definitely isn't stock paint) in Oxnard, CA

state; the chance to see vehicles that are not often kept in near-perfect condition. I took pictures of old El Caminos, older Pontiacs, and various other 'automobiles of unusual interest' with great glee throughout the time we were in California.

Old Pontiac sedan follows us somewhere near Oxnard, CA

Of course, the natural scenery is also amazing along the Pacific Coast Highway. As we drove, we saw views of the beach and ocean that almost looked like paintings, with their waves and clouds giving an

Almost looks like a painting—the view up the Pacific Coast Highway near Ventura, CA

The shot: Ivelis, Grace, the Pacific Coast Highway, & the Pacific Ocean—somewhere north of Ventura, CA

impressionistic look.

After passing through the center of Ventura on the Ventura Freeway, we exited back onto the Pacific Coast Highway. Soon after, we pulled over to the side of the road next to the ocean and I got out to take some pictures. As Ivelis posed with *Grace*, people driving by beeped their horns and gave many a thumbs-up.

After taking the pictures, we got back on Interstate 101 and continued driving along the ocean, passing through Santa Barbara until we reached Gaviota Pass. At that point we turned inland, passing through Lompoc and the outer parts of the huge Vandenberg Air Force Base on our way to Santa Maria.

Catching Up With Kevin

In the early afternoon, we arrived in the center of Santa Maria. After several missed turns in town (we kept failing to guess the directions of the one way streets correctly), we pulled up safely to my friend Kevin O'Connor's apartment. Showing an admirable and much appreciated sense for the priorities of folks who have been on the road for a while, Kevin quickly showed Ivelis his washer and dryer. Meanwhile, I foraged for an ATM and visited the local Rite Aid for various personal items. As Ivelis always says, "It's America—if you need something while you are on the road you can probably get it."

It was a nice change of pace to be staying in someone's home instead of a hotel. Kevin had obviously been planning our visit for a while and he had an array of events lined up for us. For dinner, he took us out to sample a Santa Maria style barbecue (which is definitely *not* your normal western barbecue) at the one of the primary practitioners thereof—the Far Western Tavern in Guadalupe, which dates from 1918. During our dinner at the Far Western we also sampled various excellent local wines which Kevin picked out for us. Ivelis and I found the whole process delightful and enjoyed the Santa Maria barbecue experience immensely. We finished the evening with some very good ice cream at McConnell's Fine Ice Cream of Santa Barbara and a nightcap back at Kevin's apartment.

After some much-needed coffee the next morning, we left Kevin's apartment in

Ivelis & me being ridiculously cute at the Mission in San Luis Obispo, CA

Kevin & Ivelis at the Mission gardens in San Luis Obispo, CA

Santa Maria and followed him in his Honda north about 30 quick miles though Grover Beach to San Luis Obispo. We visited the Mission San Luis Obispo de Tolosa on Palm Street first, taking a quick look inside the chancel just before mass began. The Mission is a complex of buildings, the first of which was built in 1793-1794 at the behest of Spanish monks. The Mission's buildings and gardens were absolutely lovely on this beautiful day.

Church bell at the Mission in San Luis Obispo, CA

A bird of paradise in the garden of the Mission in San Luis Obispo, CA

Kevin gave us a quick but still insightful tour of some of the other sights in downtown San Luis Obispo and then led us northwest for about another 15 miles to an excellent breakfast at Dorn's Original Breakers Cafe in Morro Bay. Along with the excellent food, our table at the Breakers Cafe had a great view of the spectacular and distinctive Morro Rock, the 'Gibraltar of the Pacific,' first sighted by Portuguese explorer Juan Cabrillo in 1542.

Morro Rock, the 'Gibraltor of the Pacific,' in Morro Bay, CA

The Corvette Subcultures

There are a vast amount of differentiated Corvette subcultures; all manner of drivers and waxers and racers and restorers and more. Ivelis and I inhabit somewhere in the middle of it all, interested in everything, but not quite giving our Corvette lives over to any single category.

All these subcultures share some constants: an urge to take pictures, find others of like interests, and, above all, an ability to forgive and adjust to much if a person is a Corvette person.

Like everything else, the Internet has changed the Corvette world. The Corvette Forum (www.corvetteforum.com) is my most-used on-line Corvette resource, though there are many others. Composed of about ten thousand active members at the time, the forum was able to help me (quickly) with several travel-related questions that I asked while we were on this trip, among them questions about why premium gas was lower octane in Arizona and New Mexico (altitude) and how to temporarily silence a slight whistle on the passenger side window (dialectric grease).

Joining An Impromptu Caravan

After a leisurely breakfast, we parted ways with Kevin and headed north along the Pacific Coast Highway. We drove along alone for a little while until we passed a bunch of Corvettes pulled over in an overlook near San Simeon. We turned around as soon as possible and joined them.

What a blast! We joined in an impromptu caravan with our new friends, about 15 to 20 folks from South Valley Corvettes who were returning from their annual San Simeon cruise. After finding out where we were from and what we were doing, they told us that we should have attended their dinner the night before—we would have easily won the prize for furthest driven (the people who won it only came from Oregon, said one of the guys)! They even gave our only somewhat dirty—it would be a lot dirtier later in the trip—Corvette a little detailing, since it wasn't quite as bright and

Two guys from South Valley Corvettes tend to a somewhat messy Grace

Following a caravan of Corvettes heading north on the Pacific Coast Highway south of San Francisco, CA

shiny as all their Corvettes were (I am not making this up).

The folks from South Valley Corvettes were all heading north like us, so we caravaned with them for a couple of hours until they stopped for lunch.

After we left the folks from South Valley Corvettes, we continued to head north along the Pacific Coast Highway. We filled up at a Shell in Big Sur before passing through Carmel, Monterey, Seaside, Marina, Santa Cruz, Half Moon Bay, and Pacifica on our way to San Francisco. Of course, we saw more spectacular cars along the way, including a Lamborghini Gallardo—the relatively low-priced Lamborghini that is causing Lamborghini's dealers all manner of unforeseen issues because some of the owners having the nerve to use it as a daily driver!

We arrived in San Francisco proper in the mid-afternoon. Traffic was busy for a Sunday afternoon, but not ridiculous as we made our way north along 19th Avenue, passing through Golden Gate Park and the Presidio before crossing over to Sausilito on the always lovely Golden Gate Bridge. On the other side, we stopped at the very crowded Golden Gate Vista Point in Sausalito (whose name is derived from Spanish for "little willow grove") and took more than a few pictures of the bridge, the bay, and (of course) *Grace*.

After our picture-taking, we continued along the Pacific Coast Highway, through Stinson Beach, Point Reyes Station, and Marshall. The northern coastline of California is massively less populated than the southern coastline. Instead of the medium to heavy traffic that we had seen earlier in the day, there is just an incredibly

Not all Corvettes on this day—we follow a Lamborghini Gallardo north along the Pacific Coast Highway

Looking back towards San Francisco and the Golden Gate Bridge from Sausalito, CA

Grace and the Golden Gate Bridge viewed from Sausalito, CA

winding road alongside the ocean, though we did drive by a fairly scary looking and recent crash with state tropers and an ambulance on-site.

The fact that the northern California coastline is more rural also means that there is more agricultural activity—and I don't merely mean wine. As we drove north, we saw several signs warning of cow crossings. Ivelis wondered aloud if these might be really lean cows because of walking up and down the hilly terrain. As if on cue, we came around the next curve and there were cows (not particularly lean) crossing the road.

Bread, Rum, & Coke

As the sky got darker, I began to realize that I had significantly underestimated the amount of time it would take to travel the 130 or so miles from San Francisco to Point Arena, where we were planning to stay for the night. Even with me keeping the 'hammer down' (driving about as fast as I reasonably could), we were probably only averaging 30 miles per hour, where earlier in the day we had been able to sustain an easy 60 mph or better. We passed all too slowly through Bodega Bay (where Alfred Hitchcock's *The Birds* is set) and Gualala.

It was about 9:30 P.M. and quite dark when we finally arrived in the tiny town of Point Arena, population about 500, nestled along the ocean in Mendocino county. It took us another twenty minutes to find the Wharf Master's Inn, which was not well mapped on any of our sources, though I must confess that we might not have had the greatest analytical and search capabilities at that point in the evening. When we finally got to the inn, Ivelis just wanted to get some sleep but I felt like I had to get something to eat. I walked down to the local bar and grill, but all they had left was bread (the kitchen was closed). At that point I was desperate, so I had gratefully ate their bread and drank a rum and coke.

I'm sure the view of the ocean from the room we stayed in is gorgeous, but we never really saw it. After a fitful night's sleep (I'll merely mention that the walls were not very thick at the inn), we got up early the next day and pointed *Grace* inland, traveling over the Mendicino Mountains along Mountain View Road and Route 128 to US Highway 101 in Cloverdale. A fill up of premium fuel in Hopland (named, I believe, for its production of beer hops) and a big, late, and quiet breakfast at Elliot's Mutt

At speed, heading through the towering redwoods along US 101 in northern California

Hut in Ukiah were both quite a relief.

We continued up U.S. Highway 101, passing through Willits and Laytonville. In Leggett, 101 rejoins the Pacific Coast Highway. From Leggett, we passed through Garberville and Redcrest before seeing the coastline again near Eureka. At this point, we headed up the coast through Acarta, Orick, Klamath, and Crescent City to the Oregon border.

We headed up the coast along the

Entering Oregon near Brookings

Pacific Coast Highway, entering Oregon near Brookings. About 35 miles up the Oregon coast, we stopped at the Gold Beach visitor's center for a driving break, some pictures, and information. One of the ladies there gave us highly enthusiastic chapter and verse on why we should stay in Gold Beach the next time we pass through the area.

We saw many tsunami warning signs along the coast—a sign format designed at the Oregon State University that has now been adopted around the world. Continuing on, we passed through Port Oford, Sixes, Langlois (known for its blue cheese), and Bandon (a center for cranberry production), before stopping for fuel at an Exxon in Coos Bay.

That night, we stayed at the Best Western in Coos Bay. Coos Bay, founded in the 1850s, is a hard working logging and shipping city that has yet to yield its identity to a more lethargic lifestyle, though there are increasingly more retirees moving into the area. Sir Francis Drake is thought to have sought shelter for his ship *Golden Hind* in Coos Bay in 1579.

Grace rests quietly across from a couple of Harleys in the evening rain at our motel in Coos Bay, OR

Dinner that night was several blocks away from our Best Western at the Pacific Grill and Smokehouse, a very relaxed family-style seafood and steakhouse restaurant with an interesting and unusual view of some of the industrial portions of Coos Bay.

Not a sign you see on the east coast—somewhere on the Pacific Coast Highway along the coast of Oregon

It was raining on and off the next morning as we crossed the nearly mile-long Coos Bay Bridge and drove north along the shore. We stopped for breakfast at a diner near Florence, noting with amusement the small drive-thru espresso places that were starting to pop up every five or ten miles. In Lincoln City, I purchased a set of penny loafers at the local Bass outlet store—the ones I was wearing were disintegrating from the effects of constant wear. Shortly after this, we turned inland and headed along Route 18 (the Salmon River Highway) and Route 22 (the Willamina-Salem Highway) to Salem.

Where I Found Lauren

By the time we arrived in Salem, the rain was really coming down. Delon BMW in Salem was a planned stop on our trip because it's where I found my other Corvette, so I jumped out of the car in the pouring rain and took some pictures of the dealership as several bemused (or perhaps amused) salespeople looked on.

Outside of Delon BMW in Salem, OR

After our stop in Salem, we headed north along Interstate 5 through Woodburn and toward Portland. In Portland we crossed the appropriately-though-unimaginatively-named Interstate Bridge over the Columbia River into Washington state.

We headed north along Interstate 5, passing through Kelso and Centralia in the steady but not unexpected rain, and following a driver in a red Corvette coupe for

My Other Corvette

Lauren in August, 2004—she looks much better now

Unlike Grace's near perfection, my other Corvette is most definitely a work in progress. Lauren, a 1985 coupe, was purchased over the Internet from Delon BMW in Salem in February 2004 after spending her entire life in Oregon. After having it shipped eastward across the United States and getting a handle on what the issues were, I started restoring it in earnest in the summer of 2004, just after having it judged for the first time. Restoration is definitely an iterative process, but every six months I can look back on obvious improvement and my scores in National Corvette Restorers Society (NCRS) Flight Judging have confirmed this impression.

Lauren is a classic example of buying the car you wanted when you were a teenager. Why the rather unusual color, you might ask, instead of the more popular red or black? For the record, that color is light blue metallic, and I have two reasons. Reason number one is that, when this version of the Corvette was new, many of the cover Corvettes on the automobile magazines of the day were this color. Reason two comes back to me: the first C4 Corvette I ever saw was light blue metallic. I worked part time at a Chevrolet dealership in the mid-80s and I'll never forget seeing that car for the first time, headlights up, fancy new metallic paint with clear coat looking its best in the setting sun. A visceral moment for a fifteen year old—the exact point where my opinion of Corvettes changed from grudging respect (I was more of a Pontiac and BMW fan) to "I will have one of those some day."

There's one more thing I think you might be wondering—where does the name come from? Lauren is named after Lauren Hutton—a classy 1980s model.

a while who seemed to know what he or she was doing.

In the early afternoon, we fueled at a Chevron in Tumwater and than passed through Olympia Lacey, and Lakewood. A little further along the highway in Washington, we stopped at a conveniently located CompUSA in Tacoma and secured a replacement automotive power adaptor for my ThinkPad X31 (the multi-purpose power adaptor we had left Pennsylvania with two weeks before had begun to fail).

After passing through the bedroom community of Federal Way, we headed into downtown Seattle, getting off the interstate

Following a Corvette coupe in the rain near Centralia, WA

The Electronics

We carried a significant amount of technology on this trip, though I tried hard not to carry too much. Most folks will think (and I'll grudgingly agree) that I probably failed in this attempt.

The first and probably the most important technology component was a small (12-inch screen, under 4 pounds) IBM ThinkPad X31 running Windows XP Professional Service Pack 2. There were

The workhorse ThinkPad X31

two killer apps on this machine, but the most important was Microsoft Streets & Trips 2005 with the small but perfectly effective Microsoft GPS receiver attached. The second killer app was Nikon Capture, which I used to download the raw images from my Nikon D70 every evening.

I also carrried a Palm Treo 650 with Mapopolis mapping software as a backup to the mapping software on the ThinkPad. The Treo also had Handmark's Express weather forecasts on board. That program has the ability to show reasonably current weather radar from any location in the U.S., so we were at least somewhat prepared for most of the wind, rain, and snow that we encountered. Finally, the Treo carried a copy of Vindigo, which helped us with locating and selecting restaurants and services in the larger cities we visited.

at Seneca Street. In Seattle, we stayed at the Westin—I had no preconceived notions about hotels in Seattle so we went with the best deal available on what I saw as a decent hotel. Though one of the two towers was under renovation, the Westin still provided us with an unexpectedly amazing view of the Seattle Space Needle (built for the 1962 World's Fair) and Puget Sound, along with a really stylish and very comfortable room.

As with the hotel choice, I had no set choice for where to eat, but I checked

The Seattle Space Needle, taken from our hotel room

The night shot that came out: the Seattle skyline at dusk looking northwest, taken from our hotel room

a few guides and made a few phone calls. That night, we took a short cab ride down toward Puget Sound (Ivelis was wearing fairly high heels) to a superb dinner at Cascadia, a restaurant that specializes in using ingredients from the Cascade Mountain region. Ivelis had their tastings menu, which she pronounced excellent. I enjoyed their very impressive mixed drinks and their à la carte dishes.

After dinner, we walked back to the hotel, had a quiet round of drinks at the lobby bar, and headed up to our room. When we re-entered our room, we were treated to an even more spectacular view of Seattle than we had seen during the day. This beautiful, almost postcard-like view closed out the third leg of our tour.

Statistics

Travel time for Leg 3, Santa Monica to Seattle: **4 days**
Miles traveled on this leg: **1,469 miles**
Total travel time: **12 days**
Total miles traveled: **4,680 miles**
Miles from home at the end of this leg (shortest reasonable route): **2,764 miles**

5 Leg Four, Part I: Seattle, WA to Des Moines, IA

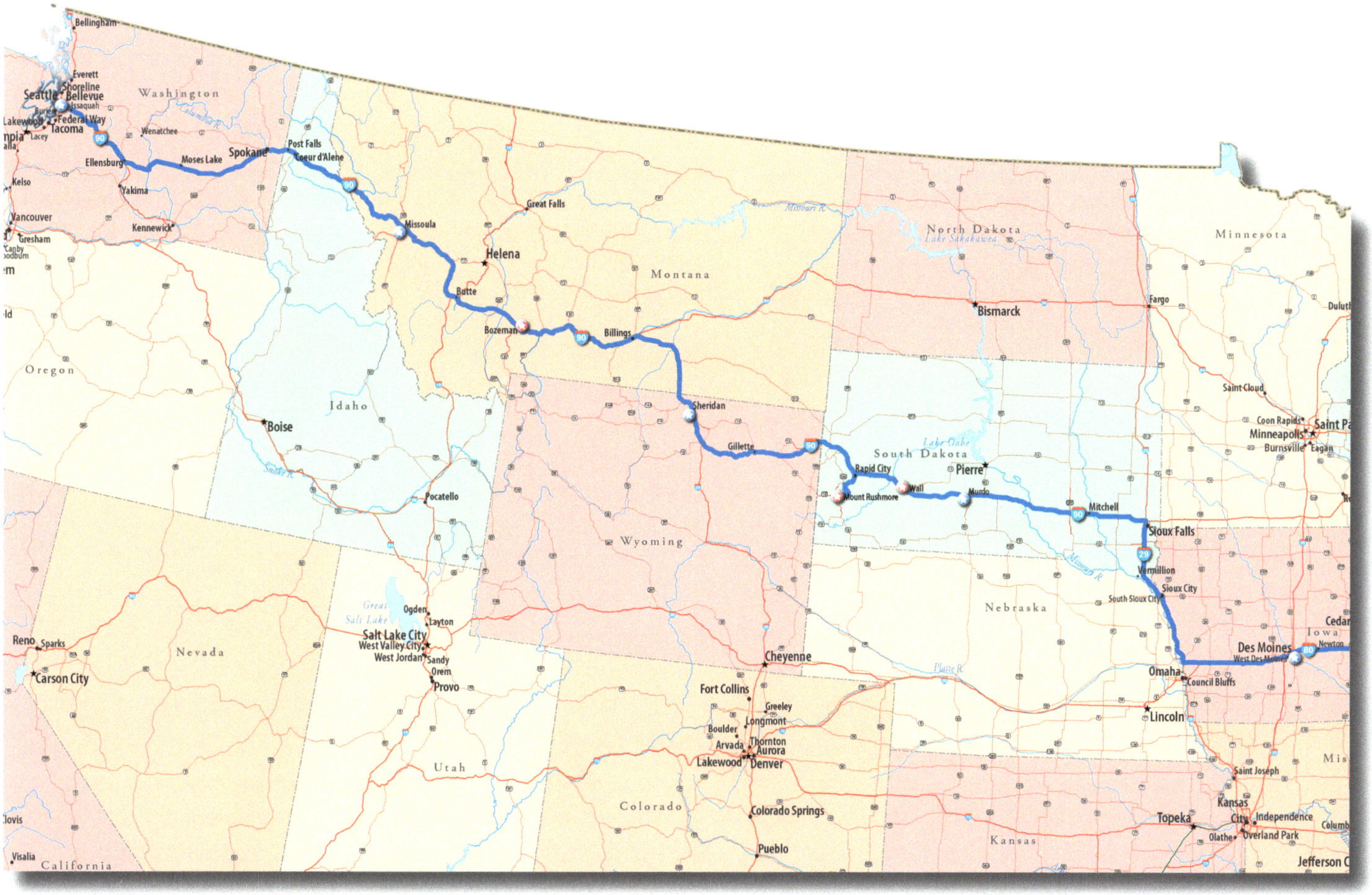

Heading Back East

We had decided to head back east 'high' (more northerly) if possible, so Ivelis could see the Mount Rushmore National Park in South Dakota. We made the go/no go decision early on the morning before we left Seattle (our backup plan if the weather looked really bad was to head southeast along Route 84 toward Salt Lake City). That morning in Seattle, the worst we were looking at in the various weather forecasts available was some rain while traveling through the passes in Montana, so we stayed with our original route.

We left the great views and the undeniable comfort of the Seattle Westin in the mid-morning, heading back east for the first time during our trip. After leaving the immediate Seattle metropolitan area, we began our travels along Interstate 90 and passed through Issaqua and Ellensburg before having breakfast in Moses Lake. We made good time heading through Washington state, driving past an unusually visible (and beautiful) Mount Ranier—at over 14,000 feet the highest peak in the Cas-

Mount Ranier in Washington

cade range. We then passed fairly quickly through Spokane (Bing Crosby's childhood home and host of Expo '74) before arriving at the Idaho border.

Entering Idaho near Post Falls

We crossed over the border into Idaho near Post Falls, where we stopped quickly for a fill-up of gas. Despite our (vast) affection for its potatoes, 'The Gem State' was another one of those quick 'just passing through' states for us—we didn't stop for anything else but our fuel in Idaho, we just headed on through Coeur D'Alene (home of a golf course that features the world's only movable floating green—the 14th hole, if you must know), Pinehurst, and Wallace (birthplace of Lana Turner) on our way to Montana. It began to rain steadily as we crossed through Lookout Pass into Montana near Mullan.

Once we were in Montana, we traveled southeast along Interstate 90, passing through Superior, Alberton, and Frenchtown before stopping for the night at a motel in Missoula. While Ivelis 'kept the motel fires burning', I ventured out in the cold, steady rain to forage for food. I didn't find a suitable restaurant, but I did find a fairly well-equipped convenience store. We ended up eating a 'stylish' meal in our room at the Best Western Grant Greek Inn—fried chicken, bottled water, a frighteningly malleable one-use-only corkscrew, and cheap (but effective) Australian wine, which we drank out of generic plastic cups.

Grace Sees Snow ... Again

The next morning, we woke up, looked out our third floor window, and saw a non-trivial amount of snow on the ground and on *Grace*. When we turned on the television, the weather people from a local television station were giggling at the mistaken forecast ... Ivelis commented with more than a bit of bile that those particular forecasters might not be ready for a national job!

Grace, somewhat cleaned off, in Missoula, MT

Bracing myself, I went outside into the fairly cold and nasty weather and started up *Grace*—reassuringly, she started right up with her usual throaty growl. I cleaned off almost all the snow, paying special attention to warming up the windshield wiper area so the wipers wouldn't stick. After this quick clean-up work, we packed up the car, climbed in, and got on the closest Interstate 90 on-ramp, which was (luckily) less than half a mile away from the motel—we were slipping and sliding the entire way to the on-ramp.

Once we were on the interstate I drove slowly, probably the most slowly I have ever driven this Corvette on a highway. I averaged perhaps 35 to 40 mph, if that. I could feel all four of the summer tires slipping and sliding constantly—and slipping is not a common feeling with this Corvette. I was quite nervous and tense, but I believe Ivelis was even more so. As we continued along through Clinton, Drummond, and Garrison and up through the accompanying mountain passes the road continued to get worse and the temperature kept dropping: 30 degrees, 29 degrees, 27, 26, 25 …

View of an icy road, somewhere in the mountain passes in western Montana

We continued on through Deer Lodge and Warm Springs, as I began to develop appropriate throttle feathering skills for the nasty conditions, the wide tires, and all that torque going through the rear wheels. After a little over a half an hour of extremely tense driving, we got off the highway in Butte, but the roads were even worse there. After uselessly meandering around that rather small city for about 20 minutes in search of either food or fuel (this was almost certainly my worst navigational decision of the entire trip), we got back on Interstate 90.

Behind a snow plow, somewhere in the mountain passes in western Montana

When we finally got through what I saw as the major passes, we took a late morning break at a truck stop in Whitehall for breakfast, fuel, and a chance to exhale. *Grace* looked absolutely trashed—the folks at the truck stop regarded us and our extremely dirty and obviously not remotely weather appropriate Corvette rather quizzically. The only person who approached us at the truck stop did so because he saw our Pennsylvania license plate—it seems he was a Pennsylvania transplant himself. We talked for a little, with him mentioning how much more open things were in Montana, but how he still missed Pennsylvania.

Grace looking absolutely trashed at an Exxon in Whitehall, MT

After a filling, somewhat relaxing, and much needed breakfast at the local Country Skillet, we returned to Interstate 90. It began to warm up as the morning went by and our altitude dropped. Ivelis and I let out a synchronized cheer when the external ambient temperature displayed on our HVAC display hit 40 degrees. The snow was now rain, which *Grace* is absolutely capable of handling, though any convertible is never as much fun with the top up as with the top down.

We made good time along the rest of Interstate 90's route in Montana, probably making up for most of the time lost creeping through the snow and ice in the morning. The weather also continued to clear. After passing through Bozeman and Billings and traveling through the Crow Indian Reservation, we crossed into Wyoming.

In Wyoming, we headed down Interstate 90 for about 25 miles before arriving at our destination in Sheridan. In sharp contrast to our morning experience of the

Entering Wyoming near Ranchester

Grace after a lot of cleaning in Sheridan, WY

same day, by the time we arrived at Sheridan in the middle of the afternoon it was over 70 degrees, sunny, and gorgeous.

Restoring Grace To Respectability

While Ivelis began tending to our laundry at the Best Western (for the last time on this trip), I also did a quick exploration of the attractive downtown of Sheridan, purchased a roll of paper towels, and made some dinner reservations.

I spent about two hours and went through the roll of paper towels and most of our remaining Griot's Garage cleaning materials restoring *Grace* to at least some level of respectability while some of the other folks staying at the motel looked on in amazement and amusement.

Eating Our Way Across The USA

One of the most noticeable differences compared to our previous trip in 2000 was the quality of food we enjoyed when we were looking for better fare. Certainly both our tastes and ability to pay for them have been at least somewhat upgraded in the last five years, but the quality of food available wherever we went has also substantially improved.

We had one of the top ten meals of our lives in Santa Fe, and the meals in Seattle and Sheridan were not far behind. I think that part of the reason is the inevitable spread of good culinary ideas from places like New York and San Francisco to the rest of the country. The other reasons? Perhaps the general spread of a population used to eating well and willing to support the expense of fine dining.

That evening in Sheridan, we ate a wonderful and vastly enjoyable meal at Oliver's Bar & Grill. Oliver's was anything but a generic bar and grill—it was a restaurant that could hold its own in far more competitive locales, with great ambiance and great food. We spoke for a while to our server Aaron, who brought out the chef, Matthew Wallop—Ivelis and I both got the impression that Matthew might need a little of the positive reinforcement we were very eager to provide.

Inside Oliver's Bar & Grill in Sheridan, WY

The next morning we left Sheridan and headed toward South Dakota on In-

Strange place name near Buffalo, WY

terstate 90, picking up some fuel in mid-morning at a Shell in Gillette before passing through Rozet, Moorcroft, and Sundance (not the Sundance where the film festival is—that's in Utah), and crossing the border near Beulah.

Magnificent Mount Rushmore

South Dakota's major attraction for us (and probably for most other folks) was Mount Rushmore. I had never seen it except from the air and Ivelis had never seen it at all. We drove along Interstate 90 through Spearfish, Whitewood, Sturgis (home of the huge Sturgis Motorcycle Rally in the summer), Piedmont, and Blackhawk to Rapid City and than drove southwest toward Mount Rushmore along first Route 16 and than Alternate Route 16. We arrived at Mount Rushmore National Park itself in the late morning.

Our visit to Mount Rushmore was most definitely not a disappointment. The weather that day was absolutely beautiful and the monument itself is quite amazing—its vast size and the way it was cut out

Approaching the monument at Mount Rushmore, SD

of the rock will impress even the most jaded visitor.

I was also rather impressed by the architecture built around the mountain. Since we were there in mid-April, the park obviously wasn't that busy, but you could see the considerable infrastructure all around, designed to handle tens of thousands of visitors a day in the peak summer season (over two million people visit Mount Rushmore every year).

One little detail at Mount Rushmore: there are mountain antelopes (not goats) with numerical tags running wild throughout the park, in part to keep the

Frontal shot of the four presidents at Mount Rushmore, SD

Mountain antelope doing 'maintenance' at Mount Rushmore, SD

Signs for Wall Drug…

vegetation under control.

After leaving the park we drove back down the mountain, stopping quickly at a small turn-off to attempt a photograph with both *Grace* and the presidents in it. That picture is on the front cover of this book.

Wall Drug, Wall Drug, Wall Drug

… extend along much of…

> ### The Beauty of America
>
> One of the surpassing truths that we were reminded of once again on this trip is how beautiful America is. From the lush greenery at the Jefferson National Expansion Memorial in St. Louis (along with more of the same in southern California) to the sparse beauty in the New Mexico, Arizona, and California deserts, to spectacular mountain ranges in Arizona, Montana, and South Dakota, almost every morning and evening had at least one or two picture-perfect moments where the road, the skies, and the scenery combined to stunning effect.
>
> When asked, Ivelis will often state that she wonders why people travel all over the world when there is so much to see in America. I agree—if fate allows, we hope to travel Route 66 again in 2015. Next time, I hope to wend our way significantly more slowly: at about 200 miles per day instead of the 395 mile per day clip we traveled Route 66 in 2005.

… Interstate 90 in South Dakota

passed through the small towns of New Underwood and Wasta.

Eventually, of course, we gave in and stopped to visit the Wall drug complex

We drove back north toward Rapid City where we rejoined Interstate 90. As we headed east across South Dakota, Ivelis took many pictures (and I took much highly amused note) of the Wall Drug signs that popped up every couple of miles as we

The Wall Drug complex in Wall, SD

in the tiny town of Wall (population 800) like so many tourists had before. Ivelis and I both think Wall Drug is one part cheesy and one part wonderful, the result of Ted Hustead's iron will and extremely creative marketing.

After passing through Kadoka and Okaton, we stopped for the night in Murdo. Murdo is a small town located along Interstate 90 with a population of about 600. It seems to be primarily distinguished by an auto museum called the Pioneer Auto Show (close followers of this travelogue will be amazed that we didn't visit this museum until they find out that we got to Murdo after it had closed for the day).

Dining At Rosie's

After filling up at the local Amoco and checking in at the Best Western Graham's, we walked over to a tiny little pizza place called Rosie's. At Rosie's, we struck up an interesting conversation with a local farmer, evidently a regular at the establishment (which is fairly well known in South Dakota). He soon brought out the owner and we enjoyed a somewhat raucous dinner with some decent red wine and an excellent pizza.

The next morning we returned to Interstate 90 and headed toward Iowa, passing through Vivian, Oacoma, and Chamberlain before pausing at a rest stop with nice views of Lake Francis Case and some rather scary signs. We got back on the Interstate and traveled through White Lake and Mitchell on our way to Sioux Falls. In Sioux Falls, we turned south along Interstate 29 toward the Iowa border in Sioux City.

Our route through Sioux City kept us quite close to Nebraska—we were within a quarter of a mile of the border for quite a few miles as we followed the east bank of the Missouri. We traveled south along Interstate 29 before joining Interstate 680 in Loveland and heading east again. We joined our old friend Interstate 80 near Minden, filled up again, and headed through Adair and De Soto to Des Moines. Outside of Des Moines, we turned off onto Interstate 235 to head toward the center of the city. We did get off the interstate one exit too late, so we ended up crossing the Des Moines River two more times than we would have otherwise needed to.

Renaissance Romance

In Des Moines, we stayed at the Renaissance Savery Hotel, a Georgian-style hotel built in 1919. Our extremely spacious and comfortable corner suite had an exceptional view up Locust Street of the golden-domed state capital, gilded with 23-karat gold leaf and completed in 1886.

View of the Iowa state capital from our hotel room in Des Moines

Since Des Moines was the first fairly large city we had stayed in since Seattle, I took the opportunity to forage for an ATM and personal items. Luckily, I had some reasonable success in this endeavour.

Sign at a rest stop near Chamberlain, SD

That night, we ate dinner at a highly regarded (and generally well reviewed) restaurant in downtown Des Moines, but I believe this was our big dining disappointment of the entire trip. This place had all the trappings of a great steakhouse (nice traditional looking room, large and enticing menu, *serious* prices)—it just wasn't that good. Service was questionable and the food was not what it should have been.

On the other hand, our experience staying at the Renaissance Savery was wonderful. I had spent just a few extra dollars on what they called the romance package, and they really delivered, with the aforementioned corner suite, flowers, champagne, and chocolates. We got so many phone calls regarding the appropriate delivery and execution of the romance package that Ivelis jokingly asked me who the other woman was.

Hotels With A History

When we are in larger cities we generally prefer to stay in hotels that have some history and age to them, rather than modern, cookie-cutter hotels. In Chicago, Santa Monica, and Des Moines, we stayed in hotels that were at least 40 years old, and each hotel was an excellent experience, with great service and lovely rooms.

There's also something wonderful about a hotel experience that isn't exactly the same everywhere you go—and recent renovations often mean that character, history, and amzing public spaces are not all you get with these older hotels: WiFi internet and plasma televisions are often part of the experience.

Statistics

Travel time for Leg 4, Part I: **4 days**
Total travel time: **16 days**
Miles traveled on this leg: **1,906 miles**
Total miles traveled: **6,586 miles**
Miles from home at end of leg (shortest reasonable route): **1,062 miles**

6 Leg Four, Part II: Des Moines, IA to Bryn Mawr, PA

Last Leg

In mid-morning the next day we left our hotel in central Des Moines, got on Interstate 235, rejoined Interstate 80, and headed along fairly quickly through Newton (the corporate home of Maytag Corporation), Coralville, and Iowa City (somewhat of a generic name) toward the Illinois border near Davenport.

We traveled through Illinois much more quickly on the way back east than we had as we initially headed southwest along Route 66. After crossing the Mississippi River on Interstate 80 between LeClaire, Iowa and Rapid City, Illinois, we turned south and followed Interstate 74 toward Galesburg, birthplace of poet Carl Sandburg. In Galesburg, we stayed with Interstate 74 as it turns east and passes through

Crossing the mighty Mississippi between LeClaire, IA & Rapid City, IL

Peoria and across the Illinois River. Sometime late that morning, we crossed the path we had taken along Route 66 on the way out southwest of Bloomington. After passing through Champaign and Urbana and fueling up in Downs, we crossed into Indi-

The Illinois welcome sign, seen near Rapid City

Spectacular view of the Soldiers' And Sailors' Monument in the center of Indianapolis, IN

ana near Danville.

We continued along Interstate 74 for about 60 more miles toward Indianapolis. After getting off the interstate in the suburbs of Indianapolis, we drove slowly along 16th Street in Speedway past the Indianapolis Motor Speedway complex (the largest sporting facility in the world), with its famous (and oft-rebuilt) 'Pagoda' Master Control Tower.

Passing the famous 'Pagoda' at the Indianapolis Motor Speedway in Speedway, IN

Impressive Indianapolis

In Indianapolis, we stayed at the Radisson Hotel City Centre. Many hotels advertise that they have great views of their cities, but the Indianapolis Radisson's rivaled that of the Westin in Seattle. From our upper floor, we had a view right down to the 284 foot tall Soldiers' And Sailors' Monument (built in 1901), with its impressive statues and reflecting pools. To top off this great visual experience, we were staying at what turned out to be a very nice Radis-

Close-up of a sailer at the Soldiers' And Sailors' Monument in Indianapolis, IN

son, with nice facilities and quite a high level of service.

After situating ourselves at the Radisson, we took some time to walk around the extremely attractive and interesting downtown of Indianapolis, traits I am somewhat ashamed to say I had not expected of this particular city. There were many interesting buildings and statues in a generally impressive layout.

That night we ate dinner at the downtown Indianapolis outpost of the extremely reliable Ruth's Chris Steak House chain—at this point we were looking for a predictable and reliable steakhouse after the previous evening's culinary disappointments in Des Moines. The funny thing was that we looked for predictable and reliable and this particular Ruth's Chris was actually significantly better than their average. We certainly had no complaints about that!

After eating a very enjoyable meal and wandering around some more in the center of Indianapolis, we returned to our hotel room in the Radisson in time to see an absolutely spectacular view of the Monument Circle at night.

We reluctantly left Indianapolis early the next morning—if our first evening spent in that city was any indicator, we'll be back more than once: we were suprised and impressed.

On the way out of the city along Interstate 70 near Lawrence, we saw one of the more frightening sights of our entire trip. It was quite early on a weekday morning, only about 7:00 A.M., and a crash had already happened on one of the inbound lanes into Indianapolis—various pieces of the two automobiles involved were still moving. This was the only automobile crash we actually saw on our trip, though we did pass two fairly scary accident sites, one on Interstate 40 in western New Mexico and one on the

The Soldiers' And Sailors' Monument at night, viewed from our hotel in Indianapolis, IN

very curvy parts of the Pacific Coast Highway just north of San Francisco. More than a little chastened by this particular sight, we exited Indiana near Richmond.

Intriguing skies & a blue arch over the Interstate greet the traveler upon entering Ohio near New Paris

Ruth's Chris did not disappoint—these Manhattens were solid 'As'

We crossed into Ohio in early to mid-morning, making surprisingly good time along the interstate—we had expected our average speeds to drop off very significantly once we headed into the more built-up areas further east. We continued through Ohio along Interstate 70, passing quickly north of Dayton, through Springfield, and taking the bypass around Colombus. We filled up 'Grace' at the local Exxon and had a satisfying late-morning breakfast at a Bob Evans in Zanesville (birthplace of Western writer Zane Grey and named after one of his ancestors). Afterwards, we headed through Cambridge and crossed over the border into West Virginia.

Preparing For Road Emergencies

I won't claim that we are ready for every possible problem while on the road, but we do try to account for some of the basics.

First, the tires are run-flats and will give us up to 200 miles of useful life after a blowout (though each mile run on them in a deflated condition decreases the chance that they will be usable for the long term once they are re-inflated).

As mentioned before, we carry a Halon fire extinguisher mounted under the passenger's seat, within easy reach of both driver and passenger. In the trunk is a basic first aid kit, along with a quart of Mobil 1 synthetic oil and four jacking pucks—Grace is too low to lift with standard automotive jacks. Finally, the combination of my well-used original Leatherman Wave and Cybertool Swiss Army Knife provide us with a bare minimum of functional tools.

Beyond this small set of tools, parts, and supplies, we more realistically rely on our AAA card and cell phones—in the end, there's only so much parts and tools that any Corvette can hope to carry.

Crossing into West Virginia over the Ohio River near Wheeling

Familiar Territory

We were in the West Virginia panhandle for only about 15 miles of travel along Interstate 70, passing over both branches of the Ohio River and through the small city of Wheeling (birthplace of famous Pittsburg Pirates second baseman Bill Mazeroski) on the way. We have traveled through this portion of West Virginia in this particular direction for so many times while returning from various road trips (Corvette and otherwise) that it seems quite familiar and welcoming; a sign that we were almost home.

We re-entered Pennsylvania on Interstate 70 near the tiny borough of Donegal. We continued on the interstate south of Pittsburgh and through Washington and Lynnewood-Pricedale, before joining the Pennsylvania Turnpike in New Stanton.

Back in Pennsylvania, near Donegal

We had made far better time than I had thought we would so we canceled our last night's reservation in Breezewood (I was unable to successfully complete a call with the Breezewood Best Western but was able to cancel the reservations over the Internet using my Treo 650—somewhat of a 'party trick'). Breezewood is noted for being the only place in the United States where an interstate—in this case Interstate 70—goes through stop lights. We headed straight for Bryn Mawr and home. Traveling along the Pennsylvania Turnpike, we passed through Carlisle and drove past Harrisburg on our way back to Bryn Mawr.

After we got off the turnpike in Exton, we pulled over and took the convertible top down for the last time on what was another beautiful early spring day.

Home Sweet Home

We arrived back home in Bryn Mawr, PA at approximately 4:00 P.M. on Monday, April 18th, 2005.

We had traveled for 18 days and 7,694 miles, averaging about 427 miles a day. 427 is a wonderfully symbolic Corvette engine size (in cubic inches) from the Sting Rays and sharks of mid to late 1960s. Amazingly, we had also averaged 28.6 mpg, despite a considerable amount of undeniably spirited driving—most of the time, our wonderful small block V-8 was barely breathing hard.

Other than a few new paint scratches and a damaged brake boot (repaired with no complaints under warranty that same month—I have a few somewhat educated guesses as to where that happened) *Grace* was fine and so were we.

Grace, somewhat battered but completely unbowed, back home in Bryn Mawr, PA

What did we learn?

We learned, that despite recent events in New York and Washington, D.C., the United States is still a very welcoming place for the traveller.

As far as us, I may be incorrect, but I don't think we'll ever travel as far and as fast in an automobile in one chunk as we did in these 18 days. By the end of the trip,

we had become fairly seasoned professionals at everything involved in being on the road, but we were also most certainly happy to be home.

Finally, this trip was a huge reminder (as if I needed any more) that I married the right woman. It was both joyful and wonderful to set out on the road every morning with Ivelis, knowing that whatever we experienced we would experience together.

Statistics

Travel time for Leg 4, Part II, Des Moines to Bryn Mawr: **2 days**
Miles traveled on this leg: **1,108 miles**
Total travel time: **18 days**
Total miles traveled: **7,694 miles**
Miles from home at end of leg (shortest reasonable route): **0 miles … home!**

A1 Appendix One: Lists

Best Of The Trip

	Ivelis	John
Best Restaurant	Tie: Geronimo (Santa Fe) Oliver's Bar & Grill (Sheridan)	Geronimo (Santa Fe)
Best Hotel	Eldorado Hotel (Santa Fe)	Tie: Chicago Hilton (Chicago) Eldorado Hotel (Sante Fe)
Best Day	Breakfast with Kevin & meeting with the San Simeon Corvettes (California)	Des Moines to Indianapolis (Iowa, Illinois, & Indiana)
Best View	Seattle	Indianapolis
Best Other Car	Lamborghini Gallardo (San Francisco)	Ferrari 250 GT Coupe (Malibu)
Best City	Santa Fe	Santa Fe
BestTown	Sheridan	Sheridan

Memorable Moments

	Ivelis	John
Scariest Moment	Navigating the snow outside of Missoula	Dropping the camera in Chicago
Funniest Moment	"Leaving already" following purchasing the boots at Back at the Ranch (Santa Fe)	Cows underneath the Cadillacs at the Cadillac Ranch (Amarillo)
Biggest Surprise	Downtown Indianapolis	Downtown Indianapolis

Post Script: What's Happened Since The Trip

• We remodeled our kitchen with a fancy new countertop, so ours is no longer the same as the boomerang countertop at Mr. D'z diner in Kingman, AZ.

• Andy and Tamiza got married (so we're *really* glad we got to meet Tamiza when we did).

• Maytag was aquired by Whirlpool and closed its headquarters in Newton, IA.

• Fuel became significantly more expensive in the wake of Hurricane Katrina and continuing unrest in the Middle East—it would have cost us approximately $134 more in gas money to make this trip in April 2006 than it cost in April 2005. I'm almost certain we'd still have done it, though.

• The C6 Z06 came out, with 505 horsepower—Ivelis threatened to trade-in funds already earmarked for our remodeled kitchen for one ...

• Ferrari announced that they would be using a version of our Corvette's magnetic selective ride control in their $250,000 2007 599 GTB. This option is now starting to look like a bargain.

•Dave Hill retired as Corvette Chief Engineer. He will now spend much of his retirement being the guest of honor at various Corvette events, just like Dave McClellan and Zora Arkos Duntov (the Corvette chief engineers before him).

Music To Drive By

We carried my 40 GB iPod, fully loaded with uncompressed music (about 760 songs) representing both Ivelis' and my tastes. This iPod was connected to the CD changer input in the trunk, using the iPod2Car interface (made by Peripheral Electronics) which allowed us to control basic iPod functions (pause, play, and skip) from the CD changer controls and provided the iPod with power.

What Was On Our iPod

Take Me Away — 4 Strings
I Ran — A Flock of Seagulls
When Smokey Sings — ABC
The Sign — Ace Of Base
Black Velvet — Alannah Myles
Karma — Alicia Keys
Sweet Love — Anita Baker
Some Kind Of Friend — Barry Manilow
409 — Beach Boys
Fun, Fun, Fun — Beach Boys
Can't Buy Me Love — The Beatles
You Win Again — Bee Gees
Nights On Broadway — Bee Gees
Tragedy — Bee Gees
Walking On Air — Bee Gees
Mad About You — Belinda Carlisle
Crazy in Love — Beyoncé
Zanzibar — Billy Joel
Rock Me Tonight — Billy Squier
Let's Get It Started — Black Eyed Peas
Call Me — Blondie
It's My Life — Bon Jovi
Livin' On A Prayer — Bon Jovi
Toxic — Britney Spears
Thunder Road — Bruce Springsteen
Born To Run — Bruce Springsteen
57 Channels (And Nothin' On) — Bruce Springsteen
Run To You — Bryan Adams
Kiss & Tell — Bryan Ferry
San Simeon — Bryan Ferry
The Distance — Cake
My Best Friends Girl — The Cars
Heartbeat City — The Cars
Don't Be Cruel — Cheap Trick
Wicked Game — Chris Isaak
Dip It Low — Christina Milian
Boomerang — Cirrus
Should I Stay Or Should I Go? — The Clash

The object of many folks affections— including ours

Drowing — Cleveland Lounge
Miss Me Blind — Culture Club
Why Can't I Be You? — The Cure
Money Changes Everything — Cyndi Lauper
When You Were Mine — Cyndi Lauper
Mary's Prayer — Danny Wilson
Bang Bang — David Bowie
Just A Gigolo — David Lee Roth
California Girls — David Lee Roth
Coconut Grove — David Lee Roth
Bringin' On The Heartbreak (Remix) — Def Leppard
Runaway — Del Shannon
Desert Moon — Dennis DeYoung
Route 66 — Depeche Mode [given to me by a university colleague in advance of this trip; thanks, Vern]
I'm An Errand Girl For Rhythm — Diana Krall
Thank You — Dido
643 (Love's On Fire) — DJ Tiesto
Heartbeat — Don Johnson
New Moon On Monday — Duran Duran
Come Undone — Duran Duran
Long White Cadillac — Dwight Yoakam
Guitars, Cadillacs — Dwight Yoakam
I Can't Tell You Why — Eagles
I Wanna Go Back — Eddie Money
I Don't Wanna Go On With You Like That — Elton John
Heartbreak Hotel — Elvis Presley
Hound Dog — Elvis Presley
All Shook Up — Elvis Presley [can you really be on a serious American road trip without at least some Elvis?]
Jailhouse Rock — Elvis Presley
Touch And Go — Emerson, Lake & Powell
Lose Yourself — Eminem
Forever Man — Eric Clapton
Who's That Girl? — Eurythmics
Bring Me To Live — Evanescence
Point Of No Return — Exposé
The Chain — Fleetwood Mac
Big Love (J3Studio Edit) — Fleetwood Mac
Urgent — Foreigner
You Make Me Feel So Young — Frank Sinatra
I've Got You Under My Skin — Frank Sinatra & Bono [stunningly swarmy delivery by Bono; I swear he's going to end up in Vegas]
Cars — Gary Numan
Abacab — Genesis
Kissing A Fool — George Michael

Another stylish Gateway Arch shot—this time a picture of the arch's shadow from the top of the arch itself in St. Louis, MO

Vacation — The Go-Go's
The Breakup Song (They Don't Write 'Em) — Greg Kihn
November Rain — Guns N' Roses
Some Things Are Better Left Unsaid — Hall & Oates *[I'm a huge Hall & Oates fan, especially when they attempt to rock]*
Family Man — Hall & Oates
Sea of Love — Honeydrippers
Amore — Hooters
South Ferry Road — Hooters
Heart And Soul — Huey Lewis & The News
Count To 10 — Imani Coppola
Lawyers In Love — Jackson Browne
The Pump — Jeff Beck
If You Had My Love — Jennifer Lopez *[Ivelis calls Jennifer Lopez one of my 'girlfriends']*
Do What You Do — Jermaine Jackson
Steppin' Out — Joe Jackson
(Just Like) Starting Over — John Lennon
Shattered Dreams — Johnny Hates Jazz
Message Of Love — Journey
Ask The Lonely — Journey
Too Late For Goodbyes — Julian Lennon
Too Shy — Kajagoogoo
The Sensual World — Kate Bush
Milkshake — Kelis
Kids In America — Kim Wilde
Stand Up — Ludacris
Superstar — Luther Vandross
Vogue — Madonna
Route 66 — The Manhattan Transfer *[we couldn't get away with only one version of Route 66]*
Honey — Mariah Carey *[according to Ivelis. Mariah Carey is another one of my 'girlfriends']*
Paradise By The Dashboard Light — Meat Loaf
Fever — Michael Bublé
Don't Stop 'Til You Get Enough — Michael Jackson
You Rock My World (Short J3Studio Remix) — Michael Jackson *[nowadays when I don't like a mix I'll try to fix it]*
Silent Running — Mike & The Mechanics
We Are All Made Of Stars — Moby
Only The Lonely — The Motels
Promises, Promises — Naked Eyes
Ride Wit Me — Nelly
Hey Baby — No Doubt
For You — The Outfield
Hey Ya! — Outkast
Live And Let Die — Paul McCartney
Motor Of Love — Paul McCartney
Ou Est Le Soleil — Paul McCartney *[Ivelis calls this 'Mulhern House']*
Radiophonic — Pet Shop Boys *[this is also categorized as 'Mulhern House']*

West End Girls (Album Version) — Pet Shop Boys
Where the Streets Have No Name (I Can't Take My Eyes Off You) — Pet Shop Boys
Games Without Frontiers — Peter Gabriel
Sledgehammer — Peter Gabriel
In The Air Tonight — Phil Collins
One Slip — Pink Floyd
Every Little Thing She Does Is Magic — The Police
Little Red Corvette — Prince [not an optional song]
Spybreak — Propellerheads
Rockaway — Ric Ocasek
C'est La Vie — Robbie Nevil
Addicted To Love — Robert Palmer
Young Turks — Rod Stewart
Breaking Down Paradise — Roger Daltrey
What I Like About You — Romantics
Avalon — Roxy Music
Force Ten — Rush
Kiss From A Rose — Seal
Morning Train (Nine To Five) — Sheena Easton
Behind The Wall Of Sleep — The Smithereens
Foolish Heart — Steve Perry
Roll With It — Steve Winwood
Edge Of Seventeen — Stevie Nicks
Talk Talk — Talk Talk
Wild Wild Life — Talking Heads
Love On A Real Train (Risky Business) — Tangerine Dream
Everybody Wants To Rule The World — Tears For Fears
The Key To Her Ferrari — Thomas Dolby
Sexbomb — Tom Jones
Runnin' Down A Dream — Tom Petty & The Heartbreakers
Into The Great Wide Open — Tom Petty & The Heartbreakers
Beautiful Day — U2
In God's Country — U2
Yeah! — Usher
Top Jimmy — Van Halen
Why Can't This Be Love — Van Halen
Me Wise Magic — Van Halen
Knight Rider — Various Artists
To Live And Die In L.A. — Wang Chung
You Better You Bet — The Who
Pinball Wizard — The Who
Oh Yeah — Yello
Delirious — ZZ Top

A2 Appendix Two: Annotated Bibliography

This trip was made with the aid of many books and references. I list a few of them below, most either travel or Corvette-related.

Antonick, Mike. *Corvette Black Book 1953-2006*. Motorbooks, 2005.

> The essential pocket Corvette reference, the *Corvette Black Book* will keep you from looking like a (complete) fool at any Corvette gathering. Antonick revises and updates it every year, but mine is now a couple of years old—stained with dirt, brake fluid, and motor oil and full of notes and extra statistics.

Hendel, Richard. *On Book Design*. Yale, 1998

> Any small amount of design 'chops' that this book may show are mostly due to reading this fascinating book that delves deeply into the process of book design as practiced by many of the noted experts in this area.

Jenson, Jamie. *Road Trip USA: Cross-Country Adventures on America's Two-Lane Highways*. Avalon, 2002.

> Recently revised, this book covers eleven (mostly) two-lane highways that go from north to south or from east to west across the United States. Jensen writes about what makes each town, city, and state passed through on these routes distinctive—views, history, monuments, diners, etc. It is impossible for me to browse through this book without getting an urge to get back on some road, if not one of the eleven in the book.

McClanahan, Jerry, and Ross, Jim. *Here It Is! The Route 66 Map Series*. Ghost Town Press, 2000.

> Out of print as of November 2006, this packaged set of eight fold-out road maps, one for each Route 66 state (even Kansas!), gives very detailed driving directions. Illustrated with McClanahan's original black and white art, points of interest, and historical text.

Schefter, James. *All Corvettes Are Red: The Rebirth of an American Legend*. Simon & Schuster, 1997.

> Quite simply, the book that convinced us to buy the C5 as our first Corvette. Schefter died in 2001 and we regret never having a chance to meet him, but he changed our Corvette plans and convinced us to buy 'Grace'.

Annotated Bibliography

Snyder, Tom. *Route 66: Traveler's Guide and Roadside Companion.* St. Martin's Griffin, 2000.

>Now improved from the version we purchased in the late 1990s, this tall, thin book includes reproductions of period maps from the Automobile Club of Southern California, with modern roads superimposed. Includes an introduction by Bobby Troup, who wrote *(Get Your Kicks On) Route 66.*

Wallis, Michael. *Route 66: The Mother Road 75th Anniversary Edition.* St. Martin's Griffin, 2001.

>A rambling and colorful book, this paperback is less of a travel guide and more one man's view of what constitutes the Route 66 experience. Still, it's definitely a legitimate part of any Route 66 library.

A3 Appendix Three: Photograph & Graphic Credits

All images copyright © John Mulhern III unless otherwise listed below

Copyright © Ivelis Mulhern
Pages 20 lower right, 21 (all), 23, 31 (all), 32 (all), 36 bottom, 45 bottom, 50 bottom, 51 left, 54 (all)

Copyright © Kevin O'Connor
Page 40 top right

All maps copyright © 2006 Map Resources, modified by John Mulhern III

2001 Corvette brochure photo on page x licensed from General Motors

Best Western logo on page 3 courtesy of Best Western International

Photo of the Chicago Hilton on page 4 courtesy of the Chicago Hilton

Photo of Nikon D70 on page 5 courtesy of Nikon

Uno Chicago Grill logo on page 6 courtesy of Uno Chicago Grill

Photo of Millenium Yellow Corvette convertible on page 8 courtesy of Dwayne Fenton

Photo of Artic White Corvette coupe on page 25 courtesy of Richard Banker

Photo of Ferrari 250 GT coupe on page 38 courtesy of Etienne Vanaret

Photo of ThinkPad X31 on page 46 courtesy of IBM

Photo of the interior of Oliver's Bar & Grill on page 52 courtesy of Matthew Wallop

Photo of iPod 4G on page 66 courtesy of Apple

www.ingramcontent.com/pod-product-compliance
Lightning Source LLC
Chambersburg PA
CBHW041533220426
43662CB00002B/47